Billy GRAHAM

Unto All the Nations

Sam Wellman

BARBOUR
PUBLISHING

Billy
GRAHAM

To Amy and Keith:
May they hide His word in their hearts.

© 1996 by Sam Wellman

ISBN 1-59310-386-7

Cover illustration © Dick Bobnick
Cover design by Douglas Miller (mhpubarts.com)

Published by Barbour Publishing, Inc., P.O. Box 719, Uhrichsville, Ohio 44683, www.barbourbooks.com

Our mission is to publish and distribute inspirational products offering exceptional value and biblical encouragement to the masses.

 Member of the
Evangelical Christian
Publishers Association

Printed in the United States of America.
5 4 3 2 1

ONE

"Billy Frank, stop your squirming. For heaven's sakes, that's why you're here."

"I don't want to see the doctor," whined Billy. He looked up into his mother's soft blue eyes. They were clouded with worry. "Oh, I like the doctor all right," he added kindly. "But I'm not sick or anything."

"Listen to your mother, Billy Frank." The deep voice had been silent all morning. It wasn't unusual for Billy's father to say nothing for hours. But it was very unusual for him not to be in the fields in May planting beans or corn or some other crop. But Billy knew when to shut up—most of the time. His father could yank him out of the chair in the doctor's waiting room, haul him outside, and whop him on the bottom with his belt—in no time. It seemed his dad had six hands to get all that done so fast. And his father didn't get mad or anything. He just grabbed Billy like he grabbed a squawking hen for Sunday dinner and did what he had to do and never blinked an eye. "Did you hear me, Billy Frank?" asked his father, not blinking an eye.

"Yes, sir." Billy felt like he could jump out of his skin. Sitting still was so hard. But his father's callused planks of hands separated and balled into fists. That was a sure sign he was about to explode into action.

A nurse called, "Mr. and Mrs. Graham? The doctor can see you now."

"Thank goodness," sighed Billy's mother.

After a few pleasantries with the doctor, in which Billy happily participated, his parents discussed an upcoming church meeting with the doctor. Billy liked the doctor. He liked just about everybody. In fact, now that he thought about it, he did like everybody. And it was a fact that just about everybody liked Billy. Was there anybody who didn't? Well, baby brother Melvin fussed at him. Melvin was the only person he could think of who didn't just about melt when Billy grinned ear to ear. But what did Melvin know? Besides sucking his thumb and spitting out his pabulum, Melvin knew nothing.

"Well, Doctor, he doesn't seem to ever wear down. . . ." His father's deep voice carried fatigue.

"That boy been eating sweets?" asked the doctor.

"No, Doctor," said Billy's mother quickly. "Nothing more than an apple or a pear."

Billy's skin was crawling. He ate sweets a lot. Suzie the cook kept a jar of sweets on the back porch. Billy and Catherine both ate lots of sweets. *Oh God, please don't let Suzie get in trouble,* prayed Billy. Billy liked her so much. And she liked Billy.

"You working that boy enough?" asked the doctor.

"He's up at four o'clock," said Billy's mother quickly. "He

goes right out with the men to do the milking."

"And we got more than twenty cows to milk," said Billy's father. "Praise the good Lord for that blessing," he added quickly so it didn't sound like he was bragging about his dairy. "Billy Frank can milk a cow faster than any six-year-old in North Carolina. The plain truth is he can already milk a cow pert'near as fast as a man. . . ."

To get it over with, thought Billy. Oh, it was pleasant enough in the barn. Smelled real fine. Hay and milk and furry cats and that cow smell. He got along fine with the cows. He liked them. And they liked him. One stepped on his foot once. But that was a pure accident. But Billy milked fast to get it over with. Then he got to go outside and feed the chickens and the goats. The chickens were just chickens. He liked goats. He liked dogs and cats, too. But, oh, those wonderful goats. He liked them so much. And they liked him. Goats were just about the warmest, smartest, funniest critters on earth. And so friendly. They even nuzzled Melvin.

"Take off your shirt, Billy Frank," said the doctor.

"Yes, sir."

"He's going to be tall and lean like you, Frank," said the doctor. "But he's got your blond hair, Morrow," the doctor said to Billy's mother. "And by dogs, if he doesn't have his granddaddy Crook Graham's eyes! They could stare right through a plate of lead."

The doctor plugged a stethoscope into his ears. *Not that thing,* thought Billy. Normally, Billy liked folks touching him. He liked it when Grandma Coffey gave him a big hug. Not that that was anything special. Most kids didn't mind their grannies. But Billy didn't even mind if Aunt Lil grabbed him and kissed him. But he didn't like the doctor sticking that stethoscope thing against his chest and back. And he didn't like that popsicle stick the doctor used to clamp his tongue down.

"Say 'aaaah.' " The doctor squinted into his throat.

"Aaaah!"

"Put your shirt on, Billy Frank," said the doctor.

Billy listened intently. It was something he had taught himself lately. Instead of just daydreaming about goats and dogs and cats and stuff, he listened real hard because every once in a while something real important was said by a grown-up and Billy realized he had daydreamed right through it; when he blurted, "Pardon me, would you repeat that, please?" suddenly the grown-up noticed him and said, "It doesn't concern you, bub." So this was no time to grin and carry on. He quietly put his shirt back on and softly stepped back into the corner, almost bumping the doctor's clothes tree, and just disappeared into the corner as quietly as Tarzan into the jungle.

"What is it, Doctor?" asked Billy's father.

"I can't find anything wrong with him," answered the doctor.

"But Billy Frank pushed a dresser out of an upstairs bedroom into the hall and plumb down the stairs," said Billy's father. "Morrow saw him at the top of the stairs. He just grinned at her like a puppy dog."

"That is a mite peculiar, all right," said the doctor.

"He knocks dishes off the *center* of the table," volunteered Billy's mother.

"And he overturns baskets of eggs," added Billy's father.

"He throws rocks at cars on Park Road," added Billy's mother.

"I didn't know that!" snapped Billy's father.

The doctor stood up. "Please, we must remain calm. Billy Frank is just going through a phase, I think."

"I pray," added Billy's mother. "Oh, how I pray. . . ."

The doctor opened the door. "I'll pray, too. He's a good boy," he added unconvincingly.

"It was a pleasure seeing you, Doctor," said Billy, grinning.

On the way back to their dairy farm outside Charlotte, Billy crouched in the back seat of the car, ears straining to hear over the chattering engine.

"There's nothing wrong with his body. It's in his head," groaned Billy's father. "He's just like my father and my runaway brother, Tom. Born to raise a ruckus. I even took Billy Frank to hear Billy Sunday last year. His powerful words bounced off Billy Frank like he was a stone."

"Billy Frank starts school in a few months, and everybody in Mecklenburg County will know about him then. We won't let the devil win," said Billy's mother. "We'll pray and pray and pray."

"But first he's going to get a good whipping for throwing rocks at cars."

Billy fumed. Didn't his mother already whip him for that? She got out that hickory switch of hers and really popped him. He was sure. He got whipped so often it was hard to remember. But he was too smart to complain. Daddy laid it on heavier then. Billy would just grin. That worked about as well as anything.

That night after supper, the Grahams prayed after the Bible reading, just as they always did. Billy Frank's mother had said from memory more than once, "Love the Lord your

God with all your heart and with all your soul and with all of your strength. These commandments that I give you today are to be upon your hearts. Impress them on your children. Talk about them when you sit at home."

But this time his father's voice trembled, tears ran down his cheeks, arms raised toward the ceiling. "Oh Lord, help a wayward child."

Billy peeked over his folded hands. Who was Daddy praying about? Catherine was a little angel, except once in a while when she ate one of Suzie's sweets. She didn't need any help. But Melvin? Yes, Melvin certainly needed the Lord's help.

TWO

"How was your first day of school, Billy Frank?" asked his mother anxiously one September afternoon. Her face had been worried that morning when she watched him get on the bus to Sharon Grade School. It was just as worried now when she watched him get off.

"I don't think the teacher likes me," answered Billy.

"What! What did you do, Billy Frank?" Her eyes looked around the farm beyond their white framehouse on brick pillars, as if searching for Billy's father.

"I didn't do anything." And he wasn't going to do anything at school, either. Not after his daddy talked to him over the weekend. If Billy ever wanted to play with his gang of goats and dogs and cats or play baseball or play Tarzan down on Little Sugar Creek or ever do anything fun again, he had better not get in trouble at school. And his daddy's eyes hadn't blinked once. Billy almost cried, "Do you mean every school day will be like Sunday?" But something told him not to.

"But why doesn't the teacher like you?" said his mother, interrupting his thoughts.

"I don't know." The truth was Billy had been so afraid of getting in trouble, he forgot to smile. He was dressed as smart as if he was going to Sunday school, but he forgot to smile. And the teacher didn't even know he was alive.

"You take her a little bouquet of flowers tomorrow."

"I don't know how." And Billy went inside to change into his work clothes. He knew he still had a lot of work to do before supper. It was a miracle the way those cows filled up with milk again so fast. On his way to the barn, a menagerie of bleats and purrs and whimpers collected behind him. *Say, that would make a great surprise someday for the bus driver,* thought Billy. He would teach his menagerie of goats and dogs and cats to trail behind him as he rode his bike. He would practice and practice. He had to use his time better at home, because school sure wasn't going to be any fun.

The next morning after he milked cows, he sat down to eat a breakfast of grapefruit, eggs, sausage, grits, toast, and chocolate milk. He thought he heard his mother say, "Maybe today will be the day when the Lord comes again." She said that every morning. There was a deep longing in her voice.

"Yes, ma'am," mumbled Billy as he wiped milk off his mouth. He thought, *Don't come just yet, Jesus. I've got too much to do.* Then Billy felt a twinge of guilt.

His mother asked, "Did you remember Proverbs 3, verses 5 and 6, I taught you?"

" 'Trust in the LORD with all your heart and lean not on your own understanding; in all your ways acknowledge him, and he will make your paths straight.' "

"That's just fine, Billy Frank."

Billy rushed outside to get his bike. He had memorized that verse long ago. Mother must have forgotten. Before the school bus appeared, he had his menagerie trailing behind him. He rode up and down the gravel road in front of the house. Several cars honked at him in delight. He grinned and waved. What a great trick. But there was the bus coming. He waved to the driver, then rode back and forth awhile. Finally the bus driver wasn't laughing anymore. Billy dumped his bike. As he got on the bus, his mother handed him a small bouquet of flowers.

"Now you give these to your teacher," she said.

And he did. He got off the bus at the one-story brick school building surrounded by a wasteland of dirt packed down by flying feet. He walked right past frowning kids into the school and handed the bouquet to the teacher. This time he didn't forget to grin.

"For me?" She saw him for the first time. "What a sunshiny smile! What's your name, young man?"

"Billy Frank Graham, ma'am."

Every day from then on just seemed chock full of school and work and fun. Some days Billy felt like he had been awake for a week. But he never got tired. When he went to bed he was asleep so fast, he couldn't remember ever trying to fall asleep. On Saturdays after lunch, Daddy might drive him and Catherine the eight miles over to Grandma Coffey's. There they played under long rows of sagging plum, pear, and apple trees. Then Grandma Coffey would sit them down to milk and cookies and tell them about Grandpa Ben Coffey— God rest his soul—who fought at Gettysburg and lost his eye and his leg, then came back to court Lucindy Robinson. "Who?" gasped Billy. "Me" she laughed. Then she would tell about Grandpa Crook Graham, who fought all through the war—year after year—right up to Appomattox and got nothing but the memory of a slug of lead in his leg.

"Grandma," said Billy, "you tell those stories as if the better a fella is, the more he suffers."

"Why, that must be your overheated imagination, Billy Frank," she said, smiling.

And it was Grandma who told him about the Scots. Each one of Billy's grandparents had ancestors across the ocean in a place called Scotland. That was way back before Washington was president. Daddy and Mother didn't seem to care. But Grandma made a big thing about how Billy's father, Frank, was a Scot if there ever was one. And Billy sensed a second meaning in her tone again. His father was not a lot of laughs. Billy never saw him play a game. He couldn't imagine his father playing games when he was a boy. He just got things done around the farm. If one of the tenants stopped plowing for a lunch break, his father would hop on the tractor and keep those big cleated wheels rolling. If anyone mentioned going any farther away from the farm than Charlotte, his father's jaw would drop. He didn't even bother to say "what for?"

Sometimes Grandma Coffey would tell Billy about the "days" when he was born. "Days?" he would ask.

"You're not born in two seconds, child." She laughed. "One fall day in 1918, your mother had picked butterbeans, then started having a baby that night. It was not until late afternoon the next day, November 7, that you were born, Billy

Frank, kicking your legs like a wild frog."

"Did they have to tie a rope to my legs and yank me out?"

"No. Folks don't pull stubborn babies out like they pull out stubborn calves."

That story, too, seemed to have a second meaning: His mother worked hard, so hard she never stopped except for life and death. And Billy had heard quiet whispers about how he was not the first-born child. There had been another child. A baby girl—who died. That scared him so bad, he didn't like to think about it at all.

Billy was like a different boy in school. He knew his parents couldn't believe it, compared to the ornery way he acted at home, but he was. He hardly said a word in class. School was just stiff, formal, boring. Maybe it was the fancy way his mother dressed him. Farm folks were like that, though. Look at his father. Daddy went all week long without shaving or taking a bath. But take him off the farm, to church in Charlotte on Sunday or anywhere in town anytime, and he bathed and shaved and dressed like he worked in a bank: navy blue coat, white pants, and a white Panama hat. So Billy got the feeling that being all dressed up put one on his stiffest, gloomiest behavior.

But one second off the school bus in the afternoon, and all that gloom evaporated. Praise the Lord. Billy felt so good, he would run around and turn off the gas valve on the bus. Pretty soon the bus would sputter to a stop; the red-faced driver would hop out and stare Billy down. Billy would just grin, and no matter how hard the driver tried to be mad, he could not keep from grinning himself.

"It's such great fun being back on the farm again and

being free," said Billy. "Even if I do have to do chores and play with Melvin."

It seemed like when Billy reached the age of ten, things just started popping. He had finally memorized all 107 questions and answers of the Catechism. And he got to hang around his daddy and Uncle Simon, listening to them talk about God. That was when Billy really learned how hard his daddy wanted salvation. Daddy was really worried about it. He went to a revival meeting ten nights in a row many years ago. Finally he saw the Light. But where was the joy of being a Christian? And had he used his life as God wanted? And was he really saved? His daddy fretting like that began to worry Billy a little. Billy just figured folks learned the Catechism, went to church, tried to remember God's words in the Bible, and that was that. A man could pretty much plan on a one-way trip to heaven and eternal glory, whatever that was. But all this fretting by Daddy raised some worrisome questions. And the Scripture from Ecclesiastes Mother made him memorize began to make sense.

" 'Remember your Creator in the days of your youth, before the days of trouble come,' " mumbled Billy to himself.

His daddy built a new two-story brick home with white pillars, landscaped in front with oaks and cedars. He even brought in city water and electricity. Billy had a corner bedroom that faced a wall of trees behind the house. The room was perfect, except for the presence of Melvin in one of the two iron-framed beds. The dairy was doing very well. Even the heads of the kids on the school bus were pulled toward its red barns trimmed in white. And they were impressed when Billy told them the farm had five or six dozen head of dairy cows, more every day it seemed. Mother wrote down figures in ledgers for how much money the dairy brought in and how much money the dairy spent. When Billy questioned that, it was the first time he really knew she had one year of college and his father had only made it through the third grade. It didn't seem to make any difference to anyone. In fact, Billy heard a time or two that ole Frank sure spruced up the "Graham place." "Has it been nigh on twenty years?" Billy knew Uncle Clyde had a hand in it, too, but for some reason, folks never saw any reason to mention Clyde. And neither did Billy.

Billy played baseball, too. He loved baseball like no other game. He loved to pound his fist into a brand-new glove. He loved to swing the bat. The swing, the crack, the flight of the ball were pure poetry. A boy could take any old broomstick down to Little Sugar Creek and sting pebbles into the sky all day long. Every one of those looping rocks was a thing of beauty. And once in a while he launched that rare comet that soared so high and so far that playing in the big leagues seemed real. When Billy heard who was coming to Charlotte, he couldn't believe his ears. Babe Ruth? The Bambino? The god who hit sixty homeruns? Yes, Daddy explained, the Babe was barnstorming between seasons. And then Billy saw the Babe and real beauty, an actual baseball blurred into the heavens. And if that wasn't enough, Daddy took him up to shake the hand of the huge moon-faced god.

"Hiya, kid," rumbled the giant as he roughed up Billy's hair.

Also at the age of ten, Billy got on a reading binge. Reading took a toll, though. It was no simple thing to tie down a tornado like Billy to a book. He nibbled his fingernails to the quick as he read about Tarzan, the Lone Ranger, and Tom

Swift. Acting out the books was fun, too. Deep in a thicket, the trees beckoned him like wizards to play Tarzan. And Billy climbed high on the branches of trees to perch above his minions. What fun it was to observe his baffled ape Melvin looking for him.

His mother was baffled, too. "How can you read books all the time, Billy Frank, but not get good grades in school?"

"School doesn't give a test on Tarzan," joked Catherine, who was never embarrassed by discussions of report cards.

Billy just muddled through. His silence in class did not help him at all. His father grunted indifference at his report card unless there was a poor grade in deportment. Then the belt came out. Billy soothed his mother by picking bouquets for her every Sunday. It was a good way to get out of the house, even if the Grahams did have a radio now and listened to *The Old-Fashioned Revival Hour* on Sunday. Because after a spell, that preaching got boring for Billy. They weren't allowed to play any games on Sunday, so Billy traipsed into the woods and took his sweet time picking flowers.

But Billy's gift of flowers was heartfelt, and he and Mother were very close. Even after he went to Sharon High School and got somewhat interested in girls, he would tell his mother about them. And he discussed himself, too. He had been studying the mirror for some time. If being the tallest and skinniest kid in his class weren't bad enough, his eyes were sinking right back into his head—deeper every year. Lately, they had darkened around the edges, so they seemed to be peering out of a cave. He almost blurted that he looked like Frankenstein's monster but caught himself. He wasn't supposed to know anything about the movie *Frankenstein*.

"And my nose and chin jut out fantastically like they do in those Mother Goose characters," he fretted.

Mother would reassure him. "Are you worried? A boy with your wavy blond hair? And your strong features? And your heavenly smile?"

Billy always could fall back on his smile. Maybe he wasn't so sure of his looks, but it seemed like kids just warmed up to his smile. So why worry? The girls seemed to like him plenty. He had even loosened up in school. Once in a while he spoke up in class. It wasn't so much fear that kept him from talking, as it was he had nothing to say. He read books all the time at home, but they were never school books. Now if they had a course on baseball, he would be a regular chatterbox. He was sure of it, although when he had to give an oral book report in class, on a really interesting book like *The Red-Headed Outfielder and Other Baseball Stories* by Zane Grey, he slouched, and mumbled, and fumbled for words, and sought a hiding place for his pipestem arms.

The older Billy got, the more sure of himself he became at high school. He began to act at school like he acted at home. Love just bubbled out of him—like at home, when he paraded his goats through the house when his parents weren't there, his humor at school was rough. He stuffed a coach's jacket pocket full of chicken bones. He helped set fire to a waste basket. The girls really did like him, though. And he liked them. Now that Catherine was almost in high school herself, she heard plenty of rumors. Kids liked Billy. Billy could have pulled away from his family at this time, feeling more and more comfortable at school. But his family didn't let him. Just because he wore white shirts and bright painted ties and ice-cream slacks and a winning smile to school didn't mean he got out of chores or meals or prayers after supper. The Grahams stayed close, and Billy knew he was expected to love his squalling new sister, Jean, even if he was fourteen years old.

It was a good thing he was anchored in his family because after he turned fifteen, his world started popping again. And with the good came the bad.

THREE

His father, Frank, was grimmer than ever. Something bad had happened at the bank. Billy would have asked him, but he knew his father was not a complainer. Besides, his father never said more than a few words, except when he prayed after supper. His father talked to God best of all, even inspired, thought Billy, but so difficult it made him sweat and tremble. So Billy asked his mother.

"Yes," she sighed. "We lost all our money at the bank. Everybody did. Reckon some kids will be dropping out of Sharon High School soon enough. But not you, Billy. We have four hundred regular customers, and most of them will keep paying us. Folks with kids won't give up their milk. And besides, what did the Lord tell us?"

" 'Watch out! Be on your guard against all kinds of greed; a man's life does not consist in the abundance of his possessions.' "

"Luke 12," she said in a pleased voice.

Billy noticed no change at all. They had lost their savings, not their livelihood. And when Grandma Coffey died, Billy could accept that. She was pushing ninety. He secretly admitted to himself that her death was thrilling. He had been right there when she rose up from her bed to cry out that she saw glory's blinding light and the outstretched arms of the Savior. She even saw angels and greeted her dear, departed Ben. Then she fell back on the pillow and died!

"She saw the Lord Jesus and heaven," gushed an aunt.

No one had anything to add. Jesus and heaven were real all right. Everyone knew that. How could they worship and pray and obey all their lives and think otherwise? Still, Billy was amazed. It seemed to connect him to the other world, the one he couldn't see. He was so thankful to Grandma Coffey.

Even when his father had a terrible accident that same year, this earthly world didn't cave in on the Grahams. The dairy ran fine, thanks to his father's hired hands and big Reese Brown, the black foreman. Frank had been sawing a plank of wood with a circular saw and a knot flew off like a cannon ball, striking him in the mouth. From the nose down, his face was all smashed in. All his front teeth were gone, and that was the least of his injuries. Frank calmly walked over to Uncle Clyde's and had him drive him to the hospital. Once there, he lapsed into a fight with death.

Billy's mother held baby Jean and comforted the three older children. "Don't you remember your father saying the Lord 'is my refuge and my fortress, my God, in whom I trust' from Psalm 91?"

By the following spring, Billy's father was back, physically fit, but not as he was before. His thin, sad face was even droopier, even more woeful. And he, too, seemed connected with the world Billy couldn't see. He was even more active in the Christian Men's Club, which had existed ever since Billy Sunday's visit ten years earlier. The men in the club decided to hold several day-long prayer meetings. And to Billy's amazement, one morning the men were parking cars by the house as Billy left for school. The men were gathering right in Frank Graham's pasture by a pine grove. Their wives were walking to the house to spend the day with Mother. And they were all still there when Billy came home after school to start his chores.

That night his father was glowing. "What a day with the Lord! This fall we're going to build a tabernacle."

"Tabernacle!" blurted Billy.

"Steel frame and pine boards," said his father firmly. "We're going to have a real revival. Get us a real old-time preacher!"

Mother said, "I heard a man at your prayer meeting implored the Lord to let Charlotte give rise to a preacher who would spread the gospel to the ends of the earth!"

"Maybe Charlotte is the end of the earth," said Billy with a smile. But his parents were not amused. Well, Billy didn't know who that man from Charlotte would be, but he was sure it wasn't him.

Billy had stretched his horizons. He was driving the family car to school now. It was a dark blue Plymouth sedan, but he drove it like a sports car, challenging kids to drag races. And it was amazing how sporty the car became when the driver had a nice tan face, wavy blond hair, and a dazzling smile. His interest in girls had advanced beyond talk. He was hugging girls at every opportunity. And the privacy of the car gave him plenty of opportunities. He remained very polite and never tried to go much beyond hugging. A few times he kissed a girl, but sometimes the girl didn't kiss back. Then it didn't seem like a kiss at all. Going beyond kissing, outside of marriage, was just unthinkable. He knew it happened, but it seemed more depraved than drinking alcohol.

He reminded himself constantly with Scripture:

No temptation has seized you except what is common to man. And God is faithful; he will not let you be tempted beyond what you can bear. But when you are tempted, he will also provide a way out so that you can stand up under it.

And God was faithful to Billy.

But how he enjoyed hugging! It seemed almost every girl would let him hug her, if no one was watching. So maybe his mother was right after all. His bony cartoon of a face was no drawback at all. After a while, he grew certain he had a charm over girls. And it made him bold. There just didn't seem to be any girl he couldn't hug if the conditions were right. It seemed so innocent, he told his mother and sisters all about his girlfriends and how they looked and how they smelled. After a while, they showed no shock at all. He could have been talking about the melons in the watermelon patch. They were interested in that, too.

So Billy had two great interests: girls and baseball. He thought he was a natural-born first baseman, with windmill arms that snapped balls out of the air like a bullfrog snapped flies. It was just a matter of time before he started connecting with the bat. Milking cows had given him a grip that could make a grown man cry. And his long, farm-strong arms blurred the bat when he swung. If he hit the ball square, the horsehide soared, almost Ruthian. The problem was that he didn't often hit it squarely.

But did Billy think that was a problem? "There's not a fool in America who doesn't know that could change overnight," he told Melvin.

"You'll start whacking it," answered Melvin obediently.

Billy was not enthusiastic when he heard some preacher called Mordecai Ham was coming to Charlotte late that summer in 1935 to hold the revival meetings his father had talked about. How would he find time to go? He wasn't back in high school yet to start his junior year. But he worked hard on the farm. And when he wasn't working, he played baseball. Or he hugged girls. When would he have time for Mordecai Ham, whoever he was?

"Too bad the local preachers won't help us," said Billy's father at supper.

"How come?" asked Billy absently, thinking about a girl named Pauline, who was just about the most sophisticated young lady in Mecklenburg County. He had met her at a Bible camp in the mountains last summer, and could she ever kiss back! A fellow just never knew for sure until he kissed a girl. . . .

"Mordecai Ham makes it plenty hot for preachers," said his father, with as much of a smile as he ever mustered.

"He does!" Now Billy was interested.

"Skins the local preachers pretty good," said his father, chewing tough beef with too much pleasure.

Still, Billy couldn't seem to make time for a revival meeting when Dr. Mordecai Ham finally appeared in Charlotte. He was far too busy with Pauline. But then he heard Mordecai Ham slurred the kids at the Charlotte high schools for being sinful.

"I've got to hear this Dr. Ham for myself," Billy angrily explained to Pauline. "It's got something to do with the honor of North Carolina's youth."

And Billy went to the revival with one of the tenant farmers, Albert McMakin. Albert was almost ten years older than Billy and had been a star athlete at Sharon High School. Albert had been down there in the pine tabernacle by the Seaboard Railway tracks before. When Billy walked inside the tabernacle, he was stunned.

The tabernacle seemed magical. The darkness was lit by dozens of high-swinging sunny bulbs. The air smelled of pine. The sawdust floor was primal but clean. There were already hundreds of folks sitting on benches and crates and chairs. And there was room for many many, more. Albert began to sit near the back.

"Say," objected Billy, "I want to be right down front."

"You sure?" said Albert.

"I'm sure," insisted Billy, sticking his pointed chin farther out.

"Let's go then," said Albert, smiling.

And they went down as close as they could get and sat right in the middle. "Why, there are plenty of seats up here," said Billy. "I could never understand why folks sit at the back." And he really couldn't understand. Shy as he was when he first started school, he had sat in the front row, silent but all ears and eyes. Billy gawked around. "How many folks are coming, Albert?"

"Four thousand most nights."

Billy did some quick figuring. "Four thousand a night for how long?"

"Eleven weeks."

"Hmmm, let's see. . .that's a lot of folks!" said Billy, giving up on the math.

The tabernacle filled. Billy had never felt like he did tonight. Regular church always seemed cool with righteousness, but this tabernacle was a pulsing, sensuous, warm thing. He couldn't put it in words. And the people. There were so many. Were folks so thirsty for the living water?

Mordecai Ham appeared on the stage above him. He was tall, fiftyish, with only a fringe of white hair and a thin white mustache. He wore rimless glasses. He had all the markings of a truly colorless man, but his face changed all that. It seemed to grow redder and angrier. Billy sat up tall so he wouldn't miss anything. He hoped this Dr. Ham spoke loud enough. He hoped this Dr. Ham would dare repeat his slurs against the good God-fearing students at the Charlotte high schools.

"You are a sinner!" bellowed Ham. He pointed right at Billy!

"Me?" gasped Billy. He slumped in his chair. How did Dr. Ham know about him? What had Billy done? Before the evening was over, Billy was shaken. He really did feel like a sinner. And how naive he had been about revivalists. He had almost pitied Dr. Ham when he first appeared. How was this singularly insignificant man going to take on a crowd of four thousand and all the preachers in Charlotte? But he had. And the fight had been very lopsided, with Billy and 3,999 other souls and all the preachers in Charlotte thrashed from their heads to their toes!

Billy went back again and again. He was thrilled by the pulsing warmth in the tabernacle and Dr. Ham's power. Billy had never heard and seen anyone who could speak like Mordecai Ham. He had heard some pretty good preachers over the radio. But in person, with all the senses tuned in, this preaching was soul-shaking. But Billy made sure he never sat in Dr. Ham's line of fire again. He joined the choir, which stood behind Ham. He was next to the two Wilson brothers, T. W. and Grady.

Grady liked to tease. "Billy, you sing worse than a calf bawling for its mama."

Billy didn't much care if the Wilson boys knew he couldn't sing. He was not going to be the target of Mordecai Ham again. Every night Mordecai Ham ended his preaching by calling folks to the altar to accept Jesus as their Savior and be born again. Of course, Billy was already a Christian. But after several nights, he began to wonder if he was really in Christ.

Finally, one night after Dr. Ham invited sinners to the altar and the choir began singing "Just as I am, without one plea except that Thy blood was shed for me," Billy felt the presence of the living Christ. Was Jesus telling him to go to the altar? Billy resisted. He was already a Christian. He was baptized. Of course he didn't remember it. He was just a baby. But he was Christian. Wasn't he? The choir started another hymn:

> *Almost persuaded now to believe;*
> *Almost persuaded Christ to receive;*
> *Seems now some soul to say,*
> *Go Spirit, go thy way,*

Some more convenient day,
On thee I'll call. . . .

Billy glanced at Grady Wilson. Grady was very troubled. "I thought I was already saved," he stammered. "Maybe I'm not."

Billy gaped as Grady lurched forward to the altar. What if Billy waited like the rich fool in Luke 12? When the choir sang the last words of the hymn "Almost—but lost!" Billy found himself trudging to the altar, head down, suddenly painfully self-conscious of his gangly height. Afterward, father Frank was suddenly beside Billy. His father put his arm around him, tears in his eyes. So his sad-faced father wanted Billy to be born again all along and never once pestered him about it. God would make it happen or not happen. And God made it happen.

"I'm a changed boy," Billy told his mother that evening.

Billy was slightly uneasy, though. He was born again, but where were the fire and joy? It had been nice in the tabernacle when his father put his arm around him. And it was nice to see how thrilled Mother was when she heard about it. But in his bedroom later, to the sound of Melvin snoring, he was disillusioned. In fact, he felt a tremendous burden. Billy felt no farther along than Christian at the beginning of *Pilgrim's Progress* as he started his perilous journey to salvation. Billy felt his imperfections now magnified. Wasn't he supposed to be already saved? Maybe he didn't really understand what living in Christ meant.

But weeks later his mother said, "You've calmed down, Billy. You seem more tuned in to other people. I know you have always loved other people, but sometimes you were moving too fast."

His mother might have been referring to Pauline. Pauline went once to the revival. She got very angry with Mordecai Ham. She had no use for any man calling her a sinner. Her life was her own business. What happened to the gentle Jesus of her church who never got angry with anyone? Never again would she go to a revival meeting. It was downright insulting and aggravating.

But Billy was changed. And not everyone appreciated it. He had to remind himself constantly not to be self-righteous because lately he had meddled with kids at school, telling them right out if they did something wrong. And he was palling around with the Wilson brothers, who went to another high school. Some kids started calling them the Preacher Boys. And it was not ribbing. It carried a small niggling hatred. One teacher even lost her temper in class and called him "Preacher Boy" as if that meant the same as "witch-boy." He was learning some folks wanted their religion watered down or not at all. If it pinched their smug lives, they became very angry.

"Blessed am I when people persecute me because of Jesus," Billy reminded himself. "That's what the Bible says." But it hurt deep inside because Billy liked everyone. And it was very hard to pray for persecutors like the Bible said. But he did.

His last two years of high school were a struggle between the old, fun-loving Billy and the new, self-righteous Billy. Sometimes the two Billys were all tangled together, like the time he saw some friends bullied in the parking lot after a basketball game. A fistfight broke out, and Billy hurled himself into their midst, but hardly as a peacemaker. He hit one boy over the head with a bottle, drawing blood. The old Billy was satisfied afterward that he had stuck by his friends. But the new Billy prayed for forgiveness later that night.

Girls still liked him, but their interest was not as free-flowing as it once was. Catherine told him girls were saying he was safe to go out with, but who knew when he might use that familiarity to pop up later and lecture them like he did to a friend at a school dance—right out in front of everyone? His new unpredictability cooled Pauline. She could tolerate his righteousness as long as he kept it to himself.

Billy began preaching to the younger children on the farm, including toddling sister Jean. It seemed a delightful game, inspired by Mordecai Ham. Where Billy once dreamed of being lord of the jungle and later dreamed of playing baseball in the big leagues, now he dreamed of mastering thousands of sinners under a big tent. "Come down and be saved," he would cry, and thousands flocked to the altar in his imagination. What power!

"I wonder if I could really do that?" he cried.

Completely spellbound by the power he had witnessed in Mordecai Ham, he impulsively went to Belk's Department Store in downtown Charlotte and began preaching on the side-walk. He waved his arms and jabbed his finger at sinners as they fled past him. Afterward, he had to admit his evangeliz-ing was a dismal failure as far as he could tell. But strangely, he wasn't embarrassed or sorry. He heard later that Pauline saw him. Their friendship evaporated.

The Wilson brothers were already preaching to anyone who would listen. T. W. was older, so any polish he displayed didn't surprise Billy at all. But Grady was a senior in high school just like Billy. Once, Billy went to listen to Grady preach inside a real church.

Before the sermon, Grady said to Billy, "I'm preaching on the 'Four Great Things God Wants You to Do.' Can you loan me your pocket watch, buddy? I've got to ration my time. I've got a lot of ground to cover."

Billy was nervous for Grady. Grady preach? He loaned Grady his watch and went to a pew to sit with Grady's girlfriend. He was amazed to hear Grady begin preaching. Grady was really good. Billy whispered to Grady's girlfriend, "That's ole Grady up there. Plain as mud." He wanted to add, "Why can't I do that, too?" All during the hour and a half sermon, Grady's eyes darted down at Billy's watch, and he wound the stem. He had to make sure it kept running.

After the sermon, Grady handed Billy his watch. "I'm sorry about the watch, buddy. But you shouldn't have held hands with my girl. It made me kind of anxious."

Billy just had to laugh. Grady always made him laugh. Besides, he was so amazed that Grady could preach, he didn't even mind that Grady had wound the stem right off his watch. Maybe Billy could preach, too. If plain ole Grady could, why couldn't he?

On the farm, the family started talking about Billy being a preacher, too. His brother and sisters were not pleased. Kids were starting to say Billy was weird. His father was not pleased, either. He had planned on Billy working the dairy farm full time after high school. And now Billy would have to continue on in some college, which cost money. But his mother was pleased. Frank was only forty-six. He didn't need Billy that bad. And they would find money. There wouldn't be enough for a truly fine school like Wheaton College, which cost an astronomical six hundred dollars a year, but surely they could afford some Christian school somewhere. She was sure of it.

"Maybe Billy will be that preacher from Charlotte who spreads the gospel to the ends of the world," said Mother.

"God willing." Billy's father looked pained to presume such a thing.

"T. W. Wilson went out west to Tennessee to that college run by Dr. Bob Jones," volunteered Billy. "He likes it."

"I never heard of it," said Mother.

"Don't you remember? Jimmy Johnson went there," said Billy brightly. Jimmy Johnson was a young itinerant preacher who had stayed with the Grahams. Billy thought he was an excellent preacher. "I would be a preacher in a twinkling if I could preach like Jimmy Johnson."

"What's it cost?" asked his father.

"Well, now you know T. W. couldn't afford much, Daddy."

"That's it then. It's Bob Jones," said his father, looking like he could make no better bargain than that. "Come on, Melvin." The two of them left to do chores.

Suddenly, Billy was out of high school with a diploma in his hand. What was he going to do for the summer? His quandary didn't last long. Albert McMakin had left the farm to sell Fuller brushes door to door. He invited all three "Preacher Boys" to come to South Carolina that summer and sell brushes.

"But I thought you were going to help me on the farm this summer," said Billy's father.

"I can save up money for college this way, Daddy," gushed Billy.

"You'll be back in two weeks," scoffed Uncle Clyde.

On that encouraging note, Billy left with the Wilson brothers to go to South Carolina.

FOUR

Billy opened his case, found one of his cheapest Fuller brushes, and knocked on the door of his first potential customer. The door opened. An exasperated face appeared in the doorway. "Yes?"

"I'm Billy Graham, ma'am. Your Fuller Brush man. I'd like to give you a free brush today. . . ." He held out the brush. "All you have to. . ."

"Thanks, sonny." The woman snatched the brush out of his hands and slammed the door.

"Say, wait just a cotton-picking minute. . . ." Billy stared at the opaque door. He never even got a chance to smile.

He learned fast. At the next house, he said the same words, smiling pure sunshine. But he took his sweet time digging in the case for the free brush. Never again did a customer get a free brush without hearing an unstoppable avalanche of words. And Billy made sure his customer was blinded by his smile. After one incident, he made sure no one popped out of an upstairs window to dump water on him, either. Like everything Billy did outside of school, he threw himself into it heart and soul. He began to sell brushes left and right. And only later, when he stopped to think about it, was he amazed, because while he was selling, he never doubted for a moment he was going to sell every brush in his case.

Albert McMakin was amazed, too. "You're selling more brushes than I am, Billy."

After a few weeks, Billy was clearing fifty dollars a week after his expenses. But he didn't save that much of it. Billy liked nice clothes, and he loaded up on gabardine suits and handpainted ties. And, of course, a salesman needed several pairs of comfortable shoes, nice saddletops, too, not clogs. One thing was for sure. At the end of the summer, he would have one fine wardrobe.

Their paths crossed with Jimmy Johnson's during the summer. Billy never missed a chance to hear Jimmy preach. One Sunday afternoon in Monroe, North Carolina, Jimmy took Billy and Grady Wilson to a jail. Facing the cells full of grumbling prisoners, most of whom were recovering from a wild Saturday night, Jimmy suddenly pointed at Billy. "I have a young fellow here who was just recently saved. Give our friends your testimony, Billy."

Billy was so surprised, he dropped his case full of brushes. He froze. He began to nervously wring his yellow-piped green suit coat he had taken off because the jail was so hot and sticky. He noticed Grady squirm. Jimmy was amused. It was an old trick on would-be preachers. "Help me, Lord," prayed Billy. Hadn't he practiced a hundred times? "Get me started, Lord."

"I'm glad to see so many of you turned out," said Billy,

remembering. Grady cackled. Billy screamed, "I was a sinner!" He was talking to God now. Did he hear a weak "Amen" waft from a cell? "I was no good!" He punched the air. "I forgot God!" Another weak "Amen" seemed to drift out of a dark, sweltering cell. He began to walk and punch the air with his suit coat as he spat out his testimony in short sentences. "I didn't care about God! I didn't care about people!" He hunkered over now, then shot straight up with each sentence. Always the arms flailed. "Finally, I accepted Jesus!" His voice was whopping back off the walls, each word as loud and clear as a church bell. Was he talking that loud? A few "Amens" made him louder yet. "Jesus brought me joy!" How long he talked, he didn't know. He was sweating; his sentences got longer, louder, more fluid. He could hear "Amens" roll out of the cells after every sentence. He felt like he could fly. Finally, he stopped, trembling in a state of joy he had never felt before. It would be a good while before the excitement wore off.

"So that's what preaching is really like," he gushed to Grady later.

All summer long, Billy sold brushes and evangelized. When he returned to Charlotte once in a while, he realized many of his old high school friends shunned him. Did he embarrass them? Was it his loud, punchy testimony? He had to admit, it was disappointing to see his own brother and sisters blanche while he was preaching and mumble weak praise afterward, glancing about as if it might be better not to be seen with weird Billy. Or was this reaction because of his message? He had to admit, a lot of folks just didn't like to be reminded of the gospel, especially if there was any mention of sin and repenting. But Billy didn't see how sin could be left out of the message. Conquering sin and death was the message.

After summer was over, Billy's father drove the boys way out west to Tennessee. Billy and Grady were chomping at the bit. They would get this school of Bob Jones cooking. First, they would take over the freshman class. They hatched a plan. Billy nominated Grady for president of the class. Grady won the election. But when it came time for Grady to nominate Billy for an office, he found out officers couldn't nominate candidates.

"Thanks, buddy," said Grady afterward. "The first part of the plan worked great."

Billy got even at the New Talent Show. He talked Grady into singing a duet. Grady frowned. "Are you sure? I don't want to hurt your feelings, but you don't sing too good, Billy."

As Grady stood up after being announced to sing, too late he realized he was alone. He managed to croak through the song as Billy hunkered down in his seat trying to look innocent.

When a fuming Grady returned to his seat, Billy explained angelically, "You were right. I don't sing well enough. Thanks for sharing your wisdom with me, buddy, before it was too late."

At first Billy thought the school run by Bob Jones was wonderful. Jones was about as wide as he was tall, snowy-haired with a florid face. Somehow he preached out of the side of his mouth, and his voice was loud and mangled. But he could preach. Still, after a few weeks, Billy was disheartened. It wasn't the preaching he heard, but the regime of the students. Boys couldn't talk to girls. Mail was monitored. Billy felt like a prisoner, his impulsive energy piling up demerits at a record pace. For the first time in his life, he had trouble sleeping. Finally, he began to disintegrate, like some wild wonderful jungle cat in a small cage. If he hadn't been allowed to sell shoes in a department store on Saturdays where he once again exercised his powers of charm and persuasion, he would have disintegrated even faster.

One day in math class, Billy realized he hadn't the slightest idea what the instructor was lecturing about. Was this a class in Medieval Icelandic? Impulsively, he stood up. "Professor, is it possible to drop this class?"

"Certainly, if you want an 'F'," answered the professor, expecting Billy to sit down thoroughly chastened.

"It's a bargain," said Billy and strode out of the room past a gaping Grady.

Billy returned home for Christmas vacation, everyone thinking he had the flu he acted so miserable. He had to be dragged along in his father's brand-new green Plymouth when the Grahams drove south to visit his mother's sister in Florida. But at gasoline stops south of Jacksonville, Billy was now the first one out of the car.

"So this is Florida," he muttered and gawked. "Warm for December."

A few stops later, he would bound out of the car. The bounce was back in his gangly frame. "Look, Melvin, Highway One. Think that's significant?"

As they neared Orlando, he was leaping from the car. "Look at the palm trees!" His arms spread out. "Look. Flowers everywhere!" He flailed his arms. "Feel that balmy air." He punched the air. "Isn't this December?" He clapped his hands. "What a paradise!"

Soon after they visited his mother's sister in Orlando,

they took a side trip to the west. East of Tampa in the midst of orange groves was the small town of Temple Terrace. The Grahams stopped to survey the Florida Bible Institute. Pale stuccoed buildings with red-tiled roofs overlooked tennis courts and a sprawling golf course. Nearby, the Hillsboro River crept along under moss-hung cypress trees.

"It's beautiful," gushed Billy.

"They say it was a former resort hotel and country club," said his mother casually. "It appears to be a fine institution to study God's Word. I read about it in *Moody Monthly*." Then Billy realized the whole Florida trip had been engineered by his mother to show Billy another school. Well, it wouldn't hurt to look. The Institute was deserted because of Christmas vacation, but Billy had no problem at all imagining himself striding across campus in balmy sunshine, resplendent in his lime gabardine suit and hot pink tie, free to smile at any pretty girl he saw. Why, he might even kiss one or two.

When he returned to Bob Jones's school, he tried to talk the Wilson brothers into coming with him to the Florida Bible Institute. They refused. Bob Jones was all they could afford. So Billy talked his friend Wendell Phillips into going to the Florida Bible Institute.

"You don't want to face Bob Jones alone, do you?" said Phillips, who was in trouble as often as Billy.

"You don't have to if you don't want to, Wendell. But I'm going on."

Jones was not pleased to see them. "If you boys don't fit in at my college, you won't fit in anywhere, not even at some tiny school in the swamps. You'll end up poor old preachers out somewhere in the cane fields." Jones ignored Phillips.

"Billy, God gave you a voice that can pull folks to Jesus Christ. You can do something for Christ in a big way."

Billy bit his nails and procrastinated. But finally he looked at the grim walls around him one last time and returned to Charlotte. His father drove him to Florida in February 1937 in his green Plymouth. Billy flourished like an orchid at Temple Terrace. The Institute had rules for no smoking and no drinking and no "heavy" dating, but these were virtues nearly every one of these students had maintained all their lives, so it seemed there were no rules. Billy felt free.

Many evangelists came to vacation and lecture there because the Institute maintained part of the hotel for that very purpose. Students bellhopped, caddied, waited tables, washed dishes, and met veteran evangelists. Billy drank in their lectures. He sat wide-eyed and absorbed informal discussions, too. Two names emerged as giants.

"Dwight Moody and Billy Sunday," said Billy reverently.

Moody and singer Ira Sankey toured Great Britain and America holding rallies so great, folks claimed Moody preached to one hundred million people! Moody softened the message of earlier evangelists into an earnest rapid-fire plea for redemption from the God of love. And Moody was a master organizer, not only enlisting the help of local churches in citywide revivals, but also creating seminaries, rescue missions, and an outstanding Bible school. And he was squeaky clean. He never let himself accumulate any wealth.

Yet, as admirable as Moody was, to Billy he seemed in the distant past. "He died before the turn of the century, way before ole Grandpa Crook Graham died."

Billy's real idol became Billy Sunday, who also preached to one hundred million people. And young Billy Frank had seen him in person years ago. His daddy didn't think he remembered, but he did. Who could forget a man who stomped his feet and pounded his fists like Billy Sunday did? Who could forget how he raced across the platform and slid like he was sliding into a base? Who could forget how he screamed at the "bull-necked, hog-jowled, weasel-eyed, sponge-spined, mush-fisted, yellow-livered, hell-bound sinners"?

And if all that weren't awesome enough, Sunday had been a real big league baseball player. He was just peaking at the age of twenty-eight, having his best season ever with 123 hits and 84 stolen bases—the most in one season ever until Ty Cobb topped it many years later. Sunday was paid more in one month than most men made in one year. And suddenly, he quit baseball because of Christ!

And yet Sunday was a complicated man, too. He was flamboyant. He dressed in flashy clothes with diamond stick-pins. Old evangelists explained how he used the pulpit like a stage actor, with a leather-lunged voice and exaggerated gestures to capture the farthest listener. But he was not just a performer. Far from it. He was as shrewd as a fox, organizing men's luncheon groups and prayer groups to help get huge turnouts for his revivals.

"How could anybody ever top Billy Sunday?" asked Billy Graham every time the subject of great preachers came up.

Fun was encouraged at the Institute as well as hard work. Billy played tennis. He played golf. He paddled canoes. He felt like he was in paradise. The curriculum was no better than that at Bob Jones's school, he had to admit, but students were urged to practice preaching and given opportunities whenever possible. The word was out: A student had to be ever ready to preach. Billy polished four sermons he borrowed from a book, a common practice. He now had what he figured to be at least two hours of preaching in his heart. Who knew when he would be called? John Minder, a dean at the school and the director of the Tampa Gospel Tabernacle, took Billy with him on Easter vacation to a conference center in Jacksonville. And sure enough, Billy got his call: He was going to preach that very night!

The congregation at a small church near Palatka numbered about thirty. Billy got wound up and hammered out his four sermons in less than ten minutes. Dean Minder deftly filled in the remaining time. Billy felt miserable. Why couldn't he slow down and be like a real preacher? When they returned, Dean Minder asked him to be the youth director at the Tampa Gospel Tabernacle.

"Me?" asked Billy, still haunted by Palatka.

"Our youth group is small and discouraged, and you're just the man to energize them."

Billy threw himself into it with his usual energy. He remembered his final days at Sharon High School. Kids of high-school age pulled away from him there. But he found these Tampa youths different. They were the cream. They were seeking God. They responded to Billy's loud, fervent prayers. And the group grew in number. Billy was thrilled that he could lead. Maybe he was cut out to serve God after all. Sometimes he wondered.

Billy made many new friends at the Bible Institute. Old friends were there, too, like Wendell Phillips. Life at the

Institute was wonderful, the most glowing of his eighteen years. Then the last ingredient to his happiness was added: infatuation. This time the girl was Emily, whose family lived in Tampa. Emily was a dark-haired beauty, pious and talented. With sisters Inez and Pleasant, she sang gospel music far and wide. She had even performed on the radio. She was not the kind of girl impressed with flashy clothes. So Billy was surprised by her interest in him after the youth group prayed for their far-flung brothers and sisters, the missionaries.

"I never heard anyone pray like you before," she said to Billy.

"My mother and my daddy taught me to pray like that."

"Really?" Now Emily was very interested. "I never heard such energy, such urgency, such intimacy."

And their romance began. Billy was eighteen. He took Emily home with him the next vacation break. Everyone liked everyone. He began to sustain himself with thoughts about marriage. Not all his experiences in Florida were warm, glowing ones. Some of his experiences were a slap in the face. Once in Tampa, he saw a man hit by a car. The man writhed and screamed that he was lost, going to hell. What could be more frightening than eternity in hell? Anytime Billy weakened in his efforts, he would think of that man lying there on the brink of eternal torture. Eternal. It defied comprehension.

The next incident he witnessed shook him to the core, too. Two very pious members of the Institute were discovered to be lovers. Uninformed, ignorant sinners Billy could understand, but these Bible-reading people knew right from wrong. He began to wonder if anyone remained true to Christ. Was all this piety at the Institute a charade? Were other Christians posturing for Christ, then delving in sin behind closed doors?

Then Emily dealt him a real blow. "I don't love you, Billy. I love someone else."

How was it that he loved women who did not love him? First Pauline. Now Emily. And he realized that there were probably women who loved him, but he could never love them. What was the purpose of all that heartache? It was so easy to slide into bitterness. What was God's purpose in having a young person crushed by such injustice? Was it to show that only love of Christ and love from Christ were true? Did folks have to suffer so much to grow up?

Night after night, he lay awake in his dorm room, now taken to sleeping on the floor to ease his back pain, agonizing over his misfortunes and doubts. Sometimes he had to get up and wander the grounds, even roaming the spongy swales of the golf course, feeling he was a brooding Lincolnesque figure but with no virtues that distinguished that great man. He brooded on and on, unable to sleep, wandering in lonely misery. Misfortunes had clouded his calling. His misery had evolved into doubts about being a preacher at all.

Finally in 1938, he sat down on the eighteenth green on a cool March night, facing the dark sloping fairway, indulging his doubts. He sat with his back to the front door of the Institute. The veil lifted. It was sudden and definite. Flickering in his mind were glimpses of rallies, throngs of folks spread before a platform higher than a throne. Yes, somehow he was going to be a small part of that. He got on his knees.

"I let love for a woman fool me. The first commandment is to love the Lord my God with all my heart and with all my soul and with all my mind. I surrender, Lord! If you want me to spread the gospel by preaching, I will!"

Billy threw himself into Christ now. He had been little more than a tourist before. Now he prayed hours on end. He read the Bible as he never had before. He was appointed assistant pastor of the Tampa Gospel Tabernacle. That was not enough. He was willing to try anything to spread the gospel. He became the preacher to a trailer park. He preached to Cubans through an interpreter. He preached on the student radio station. He stalked the streets of Tampa. No sinner was safe. Once he preached on a sidewalk in downtown Tampa, trying to save folks from going inside a sleazy bar, a certain step to hell. The bartender, discovering why business was slow, gave him one chance to leave, then whacked him sprawling into the street.

"It is an honor to suffer for Christ," said Billy, surveying the grime on his suit. And he meant it. He really felt the Holy Spirit inside him now. And a peculiar thing happened. For the first time since he could remember, he had no interest in girls other than as sisters in Christ.

He returned to Palatka. This time it was billed as his own revival. He was very bold. He asked fellow ministers to plug him now. Cecil Underwood was quoted in a local paper as saying Billy was "causing quite a sensation." Stoked by Underwood, the paper went on with flaming rhetoric that Billy led "the greatest meeting in the history of the church." Billy promoted himself all the time now. He cried from the roof tops. What good did it do to preach to empty pews? He sought publicity in newspapers. He had modest handbills printed: HEAR BILLY GRAHAM and YOUNG MAN WITH A BURNING MESSAGE. His handbills became bolder: DYNAMIC

YOUTHFUL EVANGELIST. Finally, modesty was thrown aside for Christ: GREAT GOSPEL PREACHER and ONE OF AMERICA'S OUTSTANDING YOUNG EVANGELISTS crowed his handbills.

Once he mailed Grady one of his handbills for FIRST BAPTIST CHURCH OF CAPITOLA. At the bottom Billy scribbled "Big Baptist church in the capitol of Florida. Pray for me." He never expected to see Grady sauntering down the one dusty street of Capitola. Grady had impulsively driven all the way to the revival.

"This is not the capitol of Florida, buddy," complained Grady. "Capitola is just a tiny logging town."

Billy laughed. "That's not all. The revival is canceled. The pastor had to leave unexpectedly. I'm stuck with a thousand handbills."

Grady smiled wickedly. "I'm not going to let you forget this fiasco for a long time, buddy."

Ministers around the area had doubts, too. Billy heard the rumors. Oh, Billy was already a master at praying. That had always impressed everyone. More than anyone they had ever heard, he seemed to be actually talking to God. But his preaching is frenetic, said the whispers. Billy flailed the air with his arms, bounced around the pulpit like a man swatting flies, boomed his raw North Carolina twang off the ceilings. Somehow that thin body threw out a bellow that could break windows a block away. Yet his message was not novel. It was plain vanilla. The pointing finger: "You are a sinner. Christ died to pay for your sins. But you must accept Christ to be saved."

Billy knew what they were saying: He was colorful, but it was hard to see how anyone but the most backward hick would buy such a frantic message. He had noticed the same reaction with his own family. They just seemed stupefied. But when Billy surrendered himself to Christ, it was all or nothing. This frenzied nonstop, sin-stomping preaching was Billy.

"I'm sure God wants me to preach this way," he told himself.

Still, results were what counted, weren't they? Could he or could he not bring sinners to Christ and salvation? So far he had never made the call to the altar. That was done by the presiding pastor. If Billy couldn't bring folks to Christ, he might as well give it all up and go back to the dairy or sell brushes. He was just wasting his parents' hard-earned money. There was only one way to get the answer. He had to test himself with real people. Just the thought of it made him sweat. And he was overcome with humility. Why did he, a country boy from North Carolina, think he could persuade folks to come to Christ?

"But I've got to test myself," he agonized.

FIVE

When the night for his first altar call finally came, Billy gnawed at his fingernails, sick with worry. He had prayed all afternoon for God's help. In Venice, sixty miles south of Tampa, he was going to preach at a store-front church, a converted meat market. Maybe he was far enough away to keep the stench of his failure from wafting back to the Institute.

"But I'll have to quit preaching if I fail," he glumly reminded himself. "If I can't bring folks to Christ, I'm just making a lot of noise."

One hundred people were in the congregation to listen to him preach. Heart pounding, he began. As he preached, he felt very strong. He really felt as if the Holy Spirit was helping him. Arms flailing and words exploding like gunfire, he delivered the gospel. But at the end of his sermon, when Billy invited them down to the altar to accept Christ, his heart was in his mouth.

"Now, friends, please come forward if you want your life to change tonight. Accept Christ as your Savior." His mouth was dry as sand.

He stood, hands clasped, eyes down, waiting in sweaty humility. Surely at least one would come. Oh please, God, just one. All he wanted was one. He waited. What if no one came?

Slowly a man stood up. Was the man going to come to the altar? Or was he simply leaving the church? The man hesitated. Sin and desperation were so hard to acknowledge publicly. The man slowly turned to the altar. Yes! He was coming forward. Oh, praise the Lord!

Another stood up. Could it be true that she was coming to Christ, too? Or was she leaving? She came forward. Oh, yes. Praise the Lord.

Then another.

And another.

Soon they were rising so fast, Billy could no longer count. He wanted to weep. He wasn't worthy of such an outpouring. "Oh, rebuke me, God," he prayed. This was not Billy's sermon. It was not his personal charm. God forgive him for even thinking that. The sinners came to Christ because the Holy Spirit was working through Billy. Somehow God had blessed him, Billy Frank Graham, with the power of the Holy Spirit!

"Thirty-two came to the altar," said one of the local churchmen later. "In all my years, I never saw that many come to the altar in one meeting. You have something special, Billy Graham. But what?"

By early 1940, Billy was nearing graduation from the Institute. What was he going to do now? He could stay with the Tampa Gospel Tabernacle. He was well liked, well appreciated.

He could get plenty of other preaching, like he already had. Maybe even a full pastorship would be offered to him like his friend Wendell Phillips got up in Pennsylvania.

In the meantime, he was still a student, doing all the menial things students did. One day he was caddying for two golfers named Elmer Edman and Paul Fisher.

Paul Fisher said, "We're from Wheaton, Illinois."

Billy gushed, "Where Wheaton College is located? What a coincidence. My mother always dreamed of me going there."

Fisher set his jaw. "I heard your sermon at the tabernacle. Very nice, Billy."

"Thank you, sir." Billy noticed Edman try to stifle a smile.

"Need a bit more rounding," said Fisher. "Pretty heavy on the sin."

"I appreciate your advice," said Billy.

Billy knew Fisher was studying him to see if he was angry. Billy smiled. Inside, Billy smiled, too. He really could take advice. Billy did not take offense to criticism. That was prideful. Besides, Billy loved folks in general. Only injustice set him off.

Fisher went on, "My brother is the chairman of Wheaton College's board of trustees. Mr. Edman's brother is president of the college."

"Wow," said Billy. "You must be proud of them." Billy brushed off their name dropping. Didn't he shamelessly promote himself, too?

Fisher said, "I want you to go to Wheaton, Billy."

"Can't afford it, sir."

"I'll pay your room and board for one year." Fisher looked at Edman. "Elmer?"

Edman said, "I'll pay your tuition for a year. After that,

I expect you can get a scholarship. Truth is, we want Wheaton College to graduate Billy Graham."

"So we can claim you," said Fisher.

"If that doesn't beat all. Me?" said Billy. "Mother will be so happy."

In late summer 1940, Billy Graham, like every young man in America, went ahead with his plans but eyed Europe nervously. The continent was in the murderous grip of the Germans, corrupted by Adolf Hitler and his devilish Nazi party. English soldiers, the last real resistance on the continent, were overwhelmed at Dunkirk in France and chased back across the English Channel to England.

"President Roosevelt will keep us out of it," Billy's father, Frank, had said to him as he threw his luggage in the trunk of the 1937 green Plymouth.

"Thank the Lord for that," replied Billy and drove his father's Plymouth to Wheaton. Billy wasn't so sure, though. He had read a lot of history on his reading binges.

He arrived at Wheaton College, snug off Hill Road, less than one hour from downtown Chicago, Illinois. He was twenty-two, an ordained minister, yet a mere freshman. He was a curiosity at first, the gangly, smiling southerner in his gabardine suits and bright ties. But he had something else that could not be seen: the Holy Spirit. And he knew that students who looked at him and whispered with a snicker or two would soon be silenced by that Holy Spirit. So he never flagged in leaping into every student activity. All he had to do usually was lead in one prayer, and a person never looked at him the same way again. Billy couldn't thank God often enough. The Holy Spirit was an awesome power to travel with. And it didn't hurt to be sponsored by two brothers of the movers and shakers at Wheaton College.

He majored in anthropology, which at Wheaton did not teach the student that every culture was different and that good and evil were relative, but taught the contrary. Every culture was essentially alike in its fallen state of sin, and the only answer was Christ. As usual Billy stretched his time to the limit. He got a part-time job moving furniture with a senior student, Johnny Streater.

"Say, Billy, my girlfriend has a friend I'd like you to meet," said Streater.

"I guess that's okay," said Billy politely.

So Johnny Streater introduced him to Ruth Bell. She was a second-year student, a daughter of missionaries in China. She seemed a dark-haired exotic, too. Her sharp features and wide, thin lips were softened by amber eyes, cream complexion, and complete innocence. She was trim yet rounded. She was cool to Billy. Most girls did a double take, but not Ruth. She was looking for something else in a man. Billy immediately fell in love with her.

He thought about her all the time. But he had been burned before. In the two years since Emily, he had been cautious. His interest in girls had been platonic, almost priestly. But Ruth Bell inflamed him. In his room in Professor Gerstung's home, he slept on the floor and prayed about her. He was not going to force the issue with her. He was going to leave it to God.

"If it is God's plan to pair me with Ruth, then God will make it happen," Billy assured himself.

But after several weeks, he had to admit to himself Ruth

was not going to make the first move. Maybe Billy was being unreasonable. It was hard for a girl to approach a boy. So he nervously invited her to a performance of the *Messiah*. And while he waited an eternity for her answer, he realized his reluctance had not been in deference to God's plan but fear of rejection. In all other matters, he knew a godly person carried out God's plan as best he could determine it and did not wait for God to intervene.

Ruth accepted!

He wore a new suit of blue tweed. He had bought a lot of new clothes. His southern wardrobe did not protect him from the bite in the northern air. Besides, his ice-cream suits swiveled too many heads. The date with Ruth was both satisfying and disturbing. Ruth seemed compatible spiritually. She seemed very pleased to learn he didn't drink or smoke or dance. She seemed amazed that he had not seen one movie since he had received Christ under Mordecai Ham's preaching in 1935. Her face clouded slightly at some of his stern judgments of things—but that was not the real problem. The problem was that Ruth wanted to be a missionary. Yet Billy wrote his mother that very night that he had met the woman he was going to marry.

But the more he thought about Ruth Bell, the more troubled he became. How could her goals ever be reconciled with his goals? Could he rob this godly woman of her destiny? Once again he backed off. Let God decide. He saw Ruth at student prayer meetings but remained aloof. And finally, many weeks later, he received a letter from Ruth: an invitation to a party!

"So it is God's will," he congratulated himself.

Over the months, they dated, usually going together to prayer meetings and sermons. Sometimes she went to Billy's sermons. She was strangely silent afterward, as if almost embarrassed by his sermons. Billy had to accept that. She wasn't the first one dear to him put off by his flailing arms, pointing fingers, and window-rattling nonstop delivery. Even his sisters seemed stunned by his intensity. Maybe he had been close-minded. Perhaps he could round off his southern twang, make his voice more honeyed—like some very pleasing Deep South accents. He would try that. He liked to hear that accent himself. He sure wasn't going to become a counterfeit Yankee.

Sometimes Ruth would talk of her childhood in China. It was awesome to a North Carolina farm boy who had played Tarzan. China was dark and terrible. Her very own nanny, Wang Nai Nai, had sold precious young girls into prostitution before she found Christ. Ruth had been embroiled in a civil war between Chiang Kai-shek's Nationalists and Mao Tse-tung's Communists. It was Billy's first real knowledge of the unrelenting godless ambitions of Communists. But all Chinese soldiers sounded brutal beyond his comprehension. Then Japanese soldiers came, twice as brutal. And if constant threat of war wasn't enough, there was the extreme hardship of the life itself. Unsaved Chinese mothers abandoned girl babies in the mud. Missionaries cut their own throats in despair.

Billy would gape. "You saw all that first-hand?"

Yet Ruth retained an almost holy innocence. Her worn Bible had notes penciled in all the margins. She loved animals like Billy did. Animals were God's creatures before the Fall. Ruth couldn't find a dead bird without wanting to bury it. To think of it rotting out in the open made her sick. Billy had never met anyone as fascinating as Ruth. She added another dimension to his life. But the devil was tricky. He had to be double-triple-sure she came to him from God.

Billy knew Ruth was baffled by his aloofness. He had not so much as kissed her. But he couldn't tell her he was relying on God so much. God's plans for them just had to happen.

But then he heard from Johnny Streater that Ruth had started dating other men. Billy rushed to see her. "Say, I thought we were seeing only each other," he complained.

"You haven't called on me in more than a week," she explained.

"Has it been a week? Well, you can date me or everybody but me. Make a choice."

She chose Billy. But suddenly Ruth had to drop out of school to nurse her older sister, Rosa, who was in Wheaton, too. Rosa had tuberculosis. Billy was still troubled by the separate paths he and Ruth seemed to be taking and prayed for guidance. But finally, he decided he was going to have Ruth as his wife. Longing for her gnawed at him constantly. He would ask Ruth to marry him and let God sort the careers out. If God wanted her to be a missionary, then she would be a missionary. Let God's will be done. And he asked her to marry him, but not without laying everything out front. Theirs would be a biblical marriage.

"In a biblical marriage, the man calls all the shots," he explained bluntly.

As if to prove what their marriage would be like, he would ask her what she had eaten that day, and if she had eaten too little, he would take her to a cafe and order a sandwich for her. And when she ordered iced tea, he would change her order to milk. But Ruth could be tough, too; she had seen much human suffering. If Billy complained he had hurt his back lifting furniture, Ruth would barely acknowledge she heard him, as if he didn't know what real pain was.

When the students left Wheaton for the summer recess, Ruth still had not given Billy his answer. She was agonizing over it as much as he was. Billy knew after all his dilly-dallying, he had come on very strong. But a biblical marriage was the only kind of marriage for him. And Ruth had to know that ahead of time.

Billy went to preach again in Tampa and received her answer by letter postmarked July 6, 1941.

"Yes!" he screamed.

He drove north to her grandmother Bell's house in the Asheville area, not more than two hours west of Charlotte. Ruth's parents were there. They had just returned from China. Dr. Nelson Bell was a dedicated physician and a pious missionary, but not solemn. He joked with Billy, but Billy soon realized that he was very wise in the affairs of the nation. He confided to Billy he was going to Washington, D.C., to warn the State Department that the Japanese planned a war with the United States.

"State Department? War?" Billy's head was swimming. He had never heard conversations of such worldly importance before.

Billy's world seemed to expand in explosions. Dr. Edman, the president of Wheaton College, asked Billy to replace him as an assistant pastor in the United Gospel Tabernacle. Dr. Edman was overextended. Naturally, Billy accepted. He couldn't refuse to try something new, even if inside he was trembling with doubt. If he had too much to do, something would fall by the wayside. Surely that was God's will. Open many doors and let God nudge him one way or the other.

Ruth soon visited the Grahams in Charlotte, wearing her sixty-five-dollar engagement ring. Billy's father now seemed well pleased with Billy's choices: for both a wife and a calling. "The night ole Mordecai Ham snatched up Billy Frank here for Christ was the very same night Billy Sunday died."

Billy was shocked. "Daddy, you never told me that before."

"Never seemed important before. Ole Fred Brown brought it to my attention."

"The great Billy Sunday. Imagine. . . ," mumbled Billy.

It seemed Billy and Ruth were moving to an inevitable marriage. But late that summer, Ruth's health failed. Dr. Bell thought she had malaria. He sent her to a sanitarium in Albuquerque with her older sister, Rosa. So it was no surprise to Billy when Ruth, in the clutches of depression, tried to break the engagement. That would pass, reasoned Billy. But he didn't forget to pray long and hard.

On December 7, 1941, the Sunday calm on the campus at Wheaton exploded. Japanese planes had bombed the American naval base at Pearl Harbor in the Pacific. The next day, America declared war on Japan, and three days later, America declared war on Germany. Professors talked Billy out of enlisting as a combatant. Could he kill another man? If he couldn't, he was only jeopardizing his own men. So Billy tried to enlist as a chaplain. He was told by the army he had to finish his college work first. Not only that, he needed one year as a full pastor to qualify as a chaplain.

Ruth returned to Wheaton in early 1942, still wearing the

engagement ring. She was depressed, though, sure that Rosa, languishing in Albuquerque, was going to die. But she and Billy learned Rosa had other plans. Rosa simply decided she was no longer going to be pampered. She got up, despite being warned that she would most likely hemorrhage to death, and began to attend to other patients. Slowly, Rosa recovered.

Billy found that Ruth had real misgivings about marrying him. It wasn't just depression about Rosa. It wasn't just that she would have to forsake ever being a missionary. She told him straight out that he was opinionated and domineering. And he told her straight out that his marriage would be biblical. He would be the head of the family. And she had to trust him and follow him.

"Lord, give him wisdom," she muttered in compliance.

Billy's new roommate at Wheaton was none other than Jimmy Johnson, who also decided to take that next step up in the hierarchy of religious education. And old friend Grady Wilson arrived, too. Friends were following Billy. He was now the trailblazer. And he would be graduating in the late spring of 1943. He already had a pastorship promised him by Robert Van Kampen in nearby Western Springs. The small basement church of a mere thirty-five members was in dire straits, but Billy was undaunted. He could hardly wait to get started.

Yet he had another great event in his life to attend to first. After three years of courtship, he married Ruth. The formal church wedding was at Montreat, North Carolina, on August 13, 1943. Brother Melvin was the best man. Rosa was the maid of honor. Officiating was Billy's old mentor from the Florida Bible Institute, John Minder. Ruth told Billy she would never remove the gold wedding band, not for a split second. They honeymooned for one week in a cottage high in the Blue Ridge Mountains.

When the Billy Grahams returned to Illinois, it was to Hinsdale, not Wheaton. Billy started his pastorship at Western Springs more like a tornado than a shepherd. He herded his flock hard. He was a conservative evangelical through and through, but he convinced his flock to change their denominational name to the Village Church. That way they would appeal to more people seeking a church. And slightly dazed, they followed his lead.

The original members were aghast at his sin-prodding, machine-gun delivery. But more and more people kept coming. And most important, they were drawn to the altar to accept Christ. Billy had a power to convince people to accept Christ that amazed even Ruth. His sermons were dynamic and very loud, but where did the power come from to make so many people commit to Christ?

". . .unless one admits you really do have the power of the Holy Spirit," said Ruth to Billy, somewhat in awe.

Billy was always awed, too, even scared, when he had time to stop and reflect on it. But he stayed very busy. It seemed almost overnight that he started a prayer group of prominent businessmen. He had learned long ago from his father how important support from people with money could be for the life of a church. That was reaffirmed by the old evangelists who visited the Florida Bible Institute. Of course, it was not the money Billy wanted, but what money could do for Christ. Soon he had three hundred businessmen coming to prayer dinners!

Opportunities seemed to seek Billy out. But, in fact, they found him because he was everywhere, opening doors. People said he impressed them with his dynamism and integrity. He was unbending in his attack on sin. Yes, he was brash, too. He was loud. But didn't the apostle Paul say to declare the gospel fearlessly?

Each step taken by Billy seemed ten times higher than the last. Then he was approached with an offer from Torrey Johnson. Johnson was pastor of the Midwest Bible Church. Like Billy, he had preached all around the Chicago area from time to time. But Johnson had gone far beyond that. He had learned to use the medium of radio. Billy rushed home to Ruth with his news of Johnson's offer. This next step seemed a hundred times higher than anything before.

SIX

"Torrey Johnson is overextended," Billy explained to Ruth. "He offered me his *Songs in the Night* radio program."

"But aren't you overextended, too? How will you find time?"

"I will. I have to. It's broadcast by WCFL—50,000 watts!"

"Then will you be heard all over the Chicago area?"

Billy laughed, but regretted it right away. After all, Ruth had grown up in China. "Ruth, 50,000 watts is as strong a transmitter as the law allows in America. My folks will hear me way down in Charlotte, especially since we broadcast late at night. We go on the air every Sunday night at ten-fifteen."

"Your mind is made up and racing one hundred miles an hour."

"Maybe I can get that terrific bass baritone George Shea who sings on *Club Time* to sing hymns for our program. And do you remember that quartet of young women called the King's Karollers?"

"Where do you fit in?"

"Between songs." Billy smiled. "Don't you worry. We've got forty-five minutes of airtime to fill. You'll hear me plenty."

"Where do I fit in?"

"You can help with the scripts. Just like you help me with my sermons now. And I want you in the audience." Billy knew Ruth was struggling as a newlywed. Billy craved grapefruit, sausage, eggs, grits, and toast. Ruth liked to cook Chinese. Left on his own, Billy's idea of a perfect meal was to open three cans: Vienna sausages, tomatoes, and pork and beans. And Billy was sloppy. It was a blind spot with him. He could pile things in a corner for a year and it wouldn't bother him. It just didn't seem the least bit important. But he knew mostly it was his absence that irritated Ruth. He continued, "We'll broadcast right from the church."

"Now you're biting your nails. Why?"

"Our church will have to buy the airtime. And of course I could not ask such fine singers to perform regularly for no fee."

"Your congregation has done everything you've asked of them so far," said Ruth agreeably.

"It will cost about $150 a week."

"Whoa!" Ruth sat down. "One hundred and fifty dollars is about twice what you have at your discretion, isn't it?" she asked, shaking her head.

"Even that is not really at my discretion. We're trying to retire the mortgage."

The church elders were reluctant. The expense of the show seemed to be a surefire recipe for financial disaster. But Billy, in his eager, forceful way, persuaded them. And he persuaded the singers, too. George Shea, he learned, was called "Bev." On January 1, 1944, Billy welcomed listeners of *Songs in the Night* from "the friendly church in the pleasant community of Western Springs." Then, interspersed with songs, Billy burst in over a background of distressing world news with the urgent need for Christ.

If ever proof was needed that his power was not from riveting blue eyes or a lion's mane of golden hair, the radio program proved it. Donations began to pour in to the church. It was not long until Billy ceremoniously burned the mortgage in a plate. It was strange how things just kept getting better and better. It seemed like he seldom tripped. Oh, he did trip occasionally. But his faith was so strong, he just stumbled straight ahead.

The radio experience helped his preaching. He had to rely entirely on his voice and the message. Now when he preached, he was not quite so frantic. But he didn't abandon his exaggerated gestures when he preached from the pulpit. He was no fool. Preaching from a pulpit and preaching on the radio required different techniques. A crowd seeing a preacher appreciated larger-than-life gestures. He was sure of that.

Once again Torrey Johnson called on him. Torrey rented a concert hall. He wanted Billy to be his principal speaker at a rally for soldiers he called "Chicagoland Youth for Christ." Billy hesitated. He doubted Johnson could muster much of an audience. But that wasn't what really bothered him. It was one of Billy's few dark moments, one of those moments of crippling chest-tightening, dry-mouthed, lip-quivering doubt. He had a rare seizure of stage fright.

"I must not ever neglect Christ because I am afraid to fail," he chided himself. What had he ever done to even remotely resemble the apostle Paul's trials and tribulations?

He accepted the invitation to preach. He walked out to face a concert hall that was packed with very tough, very cynical soldiers. He started to preach, still shaky as he watched some soldiers fidget. He was operating on faith that the Holy Spirit would take over. He did. When the talk was over, forty-two soldiers came to Christ. Torrey Johnson was so pleased, he said he was going to hold a rally every Saturday night.

Ten days later, June 6, 1944, the military forces of America and its allies invaded France at Normandy. Surely, the war would be over soon. But the Germans were ferocious fighters. President Roosevelt used his "fireside" radio broadcast to offer a prayer:

> *Almighty God: Our sons, pride of our nation, this day have set upon a mighty endeavor, a struggle to preserve our Republic, our religion and our civilization, and to set free a suffering humanity. Lead them straight and true; give strength to their arms, stoutness to their hearts, and steadfastness in their faith. They will need thy blessing. . . .*

"Magnificent. Shades of Lincoln," said Billy in admiration. "What a powerful voice the presidency could be for Christ." During Billy's lifetime, religion had been muted from the White House. Roosevelt had opened his eyes. Why couldn't the presidency be used to advocate salvation?

Torrey Johnson's Chicago rally had been so successful, others followed, not only for soldiers but young people in general. And not only to those youth in the Chicago area, but young people nationwide. Eventually, Billy was preaching to crowds of ten thousand, and one time, to sixteen thousand. It happened so fast, he never had a chance to be overwhelmed by the immensity of what he was doing. Torrey Johnson had him traveling, too, making arrangements for the next rally and talking to participants. Billy knew Ruth was suffering. But she joked once she would rather have a little of him than a lot of anybody else. What else could he do? The Youth for Christ movement was snowballing into something very big.

"But don't you need a follow-up?" asked Ruth. "Who's taking care of these babes in Christ?" Billy had no answer.

When Billy got the mumps so severely he was bedridden for six weeks, often delirious, it seemed his illness was divine intervention. He had just completed his one year of pastoring. It was time to go into the army. But the army told him he could never go on active duty as a chaplain now, not with his recent medical problems. So he remained to pastor the Village Church at Western Springs, broadcast *Songs of the Night,* and make arrangements to speak at Torrey Johnson's enormous rallies for youth.

By early 1945, Billy was so busy with Johnson's rallies, it was obvious he could no longer pastor the Village Church. The truth was that he had never seen the Western Springs calling as permanent. And he had told them that. They had known from the beginning he would pastor for one year, then apply again to be a chaplain in the army.

Ruth reassured him, "You're leaving the church members much better off than they had been before."

So he left the church and began to work full time for Torrey Johnson. No one was more disappointed in the change of direction than Billy's parents. They faithfully listened to *Songs in the Night* on the radio. Ruth had encouraged the change. Was Billy going to be an evangelist or a pastor? She thought it was impossible to be both. But evangelism for Billy and Ruth was a double-edged sword. Preaching and planning Johnson's rallies for youth required him to travel constantly. And there was not enough money to pay for a wife's expenses, so Ruth could not travel with him. Billy was home so rarely, Ruth left Illinois to go live with her parents in Montreat!

Billy was not worried. People in Christ had to do such things. Ruth, too, was such a person. And she herself had told Billy that Livingstone, the great missionary to Africa, had been away from his wife, Mary, more than he had been with her. Mary Livingstone had lived with one set of parents, then another. It was not a happy situation, but service for Christ was no picnic.

Besides, America was at war. A fearful reminder of the ever-present danger was the death of President Roosevelt in April. Billy not only mourned the dead president but prayed for his successor, a laconic straightlaced Missourian named Harry Truman. Was Truman tough enough to finish the biggest job in the world?

On Memorial Day 1945, Torrey Johnson outdid himself; he packed Soldier Field in Chicago with seventy thousand youths! Billy wasn't selected to preach at that rally, but for two years, he had been preaching to audiences that once he would not have dared to imagine. The results of the rallies were so promising, Torrey Johnson could wait no longer. "We are gathering evangelical youth leaders from all across America, Billy."

Six hundred leaders showed up at Winona Lake in

Indiana to formally start an international organization called Youth for Christ. To no one's surprise, Torrey Johnson was elected president. Billy became the single field representative for the new organization. Once again life changed drastically. He came to know airports everywhere. His office was five miles up in the sky. He lived out of a suitcase. He learned to wear only blues and grays so he would only need black shoes. But when he preached, he wore bright, outrageous colors to please young people. Billy was going to be twenty-seven that fall. He was known in the Chicago area to many evangelicals, and he was becoming known nationwide to evangelical leaders. Would he ever be known in his own home again?

He ached for home now. Ruth was pregnant. He tried to make amends to Ruth on sporadic visits to Montreat. Yet, somehow the Youth for Christ movement seemed always to be at hand. In the summer of 1945, he spoke at Asheville, near Montreat. His usual song leader was not there, so Billy accepted the offer of help from a pair of honeymooners in the audience, Cliff Barrows and his wife. They far surpassed adequate. They not only sang and told jokes, but Cliff played the trombone and his wife the piano. Husky Cliff rivaled Billy in sincerity and zeal.

Billy told Cliff, "I would never use other song leaders if you and your wife were around."

"Keep us in mind then, Billy," replied Cliff.

The Germans surrendered. But it seemed the war with the fanatical Japanese might go on for years. Then America suddenly dropped two bombs of incomprehensible power. They were called "atomic" bombs. One atomic bomb could devastate an entire city! Within days, the war was over. Over ten million young Americans were in uniform. Men and women would soon be flooding back to resume their lives. It seemed a turning point for everyone. What was the next step in postwar America?

Ruth gave birth to a daughter September 21. They named her Virginia after Ruth's younger sister, but Ruth nicknamed her GiGi, which was Chinese for "sister." Billy was not there. The die seemed cast. Billy was as ephemeral at home as a sea captain. The Youth for Christ movement was a national phenomenon by early 1946. Billy was relieved to hear that President Truman praised it. *Time* magazine ran a story on it. The newspaper empire of William Randolph Hearst assigned one reporter to it. Hearst wanted his large-city newspapers not only to cover the movement but, in journalistic jargon for promoting something, to "puff" it. Hearst said he liked the moral underpinning it gave youth. Cynics said he just wanted to sell newspapers. By now the Youth for Christ organization was making its first efforts to enlist local clergy to counsel converts. That made a revival much more difficult. Advance planning was a very big part now. And that was Billy's job.

Also by 1946, Torrey Johnson decided it was time the organization truly became international. Teams left for Japan, Korea, China, India, Africa, and Australia. Another team left for England in March: Torrey Johnson himself, singer Stratton Shufelt, and the organization's two most dynamic speakers, Chuck Templeton and Billy. Accompanying them was Wesley Hartzell, one of the Hearst reporters.

English clerics were appalled by Billy. They had no clerics who preached in bright red bow ties. Their clerics did not stalk the platform, bending down, bolting upright, flailing their arms. They had no clerics who spoke at the rate of 240 words per minute, never using an adjective or an adverb. His simple message of sin and salvation spattered the audience like machine-gun fire. There was no escape. Most stunning of all was the stream of sinners coming to the altar after he called them.

"I've never seen such a response before," the skeptics would admit to him afterward.

Even though the troupe had to create an agenda from scratch, they managed to speak to one hundred thousand British and Irish people in three weeks. And they made friends who would help them in future visits. They went on to Europe, where they had far more success creating a network of Youth for Christ groups among American occupation troops than converting the natives. The foreign languages and liberal theologies were a quagmire for Billy.

But he returned in fall 1946 to Britain and Ireland, this time for six months. His song leaders were Cliff Barrows and his wife. In the back of his mind, Billy felt like he was building a team. The itinerary had been arranged by a Scottish evangelist, Gavin Hamilton. Later, Ruth was to meet Billy in London and accompany him for part of the trip. But Billy's first efforts were in Wales. It was so bitterly cold in Britain that winter, the Americans slept in their clothes. And doubt froze Billy's heart like an icy wind.

At Pontypridd, a mining town of twenty thousand souls, Billy met Stephen Olford, a Welshman. Billy was as blunt as usual. "I heard you preach in London last week."

Olford blinked. "I remember you, Yank. You were wearing a pink suit." His voice carried little respect.

"You are filled with the Holy Spirit, Stephen. I want the fullness of the Spirit, too." Billy was in the grips of one of his dark moments. The Welsh were so gifted at preaching. What did he have to offer? His first sermons to them had failed to move them. Almost no one came to the altar.

The two secluded themselves in a hotel room to pray and pour over the Bible. Olford taught Billy to use "quiet time" every day to completely absorb the reality of Holy Scripture. He next urged Billy consciously to surrender hourly to the sovereignty of Christ and the absolute authority of the Bible.

"This will bring the fullness of the Holy Spirit," counseled Olford again and again for two days.

Billy believed him totally. "This is the turning point of my ministry," he cried.

That night he spoke to his largest audience in Wales yet. Before his two-day session with Olford, he would have panicked but delivered a passably good sermon anyway. Now, the unusually large turnout seemed God's direct will. His sermon was on Belshazzar's feast in the book of Daniel. He still spoke fast. He still prowled the pulpit with an open Bible. His pointed finger blasted every sinner in his audience:

> *"(You) have not humbled yourself, though you knew all this. Instead, you have set yourself up against the Lord of heaven. . . . You did not honor the God who holds in his hand your life and all your ways."*

Tonight there seemed more real authority in his voice. He was speaking for God. Daniel 5 came alive. Finally, he invited the Welsh sinners to come to Christ.

Stephen Olford was shocked. "Virtually the entire audience is coming to the altar!" he gasped.

Billy's next great test was in Birmingham. Its one million inhabitants seemed ripe for conversion; church attendance was notoriously low. Hamilton had arranged a meeting with the mayor and a ten-day campaign. But local clergy had panicked. They did not want to be tainted by these Americans and their loud clothes and machine-gun harangues from the pulpit. Besides, they had heard of American evangelists like Mordecai Ham who glorified themselves by skinning the local clergy. Church attendance would become even worse. The clergy not only backed off but influenced the mayor to snub the newcomers and cancel the use of the city auditorium for the campaign.

But Billy had learned a valuable lesson working for Torrey Johnson. Campaigning should enlist the local clergy. The converts had to be counseled after they came to Christ and turned over to the local churches. So after the first sermon, which drew a paltry two hundred people, Billy hunkered down in his hotel room with the telephone.

His calls to the clergymen were not bitter diatribes but humble appeals for help. Billy never got angry at opposition. Only gross injustice angered him. These local clergy were timid. One by one, he melted their resistance. Before long the campaign was restored. Two thousand five hundred seats in the city auditorium were full every night. The mayor received him for tea.

"Listen to this," said Cliff Barrows one morning, brandishing a newspaper. "The paper says Youth for Christ is the greatest spiritual revival Birmingham has experienced in a generation!"

"And we were almost shut out," said Billy. "Praise the Lord."

By the end of his trip in March 1947, Billy and his troupe

had spoken at 360 meetings, with major incursions into Manchester, Birmingham, Belfast, and London. And Ruth had traveled with him for a couple of weeks. Billy was amazed when the Irish press attacked her for wearing makeup. He couldn't imagine a more pious woman for the times than Ruth.

Billy had also run short of money a couple of times. He discovered he now might have to call on rich benefactors in emergencies. Once he appealed to Alfred Owen, a rich industrialist in Birmingham. Another time he appealed to R. G. LeTourneau, an American millionaire who had been kind enough to pay Grady Wilson's way at Wheaton College. Both appeals by Billy were granted promptly.

Billy wanted to work American cities like he had worked Birmingham. He started in Grand Rapids, Michigan. By the fall, he was to be in Charlotte. At Billy's city-wide campaign in Minneapolis, eighty-six-year-old William Riley pestered him "like the persistent widow" to become president of Riley's Northwestern Bible Schools. Billy refused. He had no time for that. Riley just wouldn't let up. So to silence him, Billy promised Riley to assume the role of presidency if anything happened to Riley within a year. Then he forgot about it.

"We've got to get ready for Charlotte," he said nervously.

The preparation for Charlotte was another of Billy's black moments. What if he failed in his own backyard? Even the Savior had been frustrated in his hometown of Nazareth. So Billy chewed his nails and spurred an advance campaign that went far beyond the usual billboards, bumper stickers, radio commercials, and placards in busses and windows. Billy had airplanes zooming over Charlotte, trailing banners and dropping leaflets. He gave daily press releases to thirty-one local papers. He advertised variety acts, even a race run by well-known miler Gil Dodds. He made sure Cliff Barrows and his wife were with him. He asked Bev Shea to sing for the campaign. He hired Grady Wilson to help out, even though it was Grady's brother, T. W., who evangelized full-time for the Youth for Christ. Grady was married now, with his own ministry in South Carolina. But Billy always felt better with Grady around. Grady had grown plump but was still just as quick-witted and sharp-tongued. All he had to do was tell everyone about "Capitola" to keep Billy's feet on the ground. Billy loved Grady.

Billy prayed, "Lord, don't let me fail in my own backyard."

In eighteen services at Charlotte, they drew forty-two thousand people. And as usual, if the people could be garnered, Billy could persuade a good many of them to come to Christ. Billy was very pleased with his team of the Barrowses, Bev Shea, and Grady Wilson. The team performed wonderfully well. And he had started a first in his sermons: He began relentlessly to hammer away at the threat of Communism. Billy knew the Russians had forced their godless way of life on all the countries of eastern Europe. Communism was dreary and hopeless, deliberately separated from God. But in England he noticed many people accepted this vile form of atheism as a perfectly legitimate form of government. He must warn Americans against it.

Billy felt so good about his team now and his message, he began more and more to think about going out on his own to evangelize. Then on December 6, 1947, while he was evangelizing for Youth for Christ in Hattiesburg, Mississippi, he got a phone call.

After he listened to the voice on the phone, Billy had to sit down, stunned.

SEVEN

Billy was shocked. He called Ruth. "William Riley died."
"May he rest in peace." Ruth sighed. "You promised."

Since spring 1945, Billy had traveled to forty-seven states
for Youth for Christ. He had flown over two hundred thousand
miles. One year United Airlines tabbed him their most frequent flyer. He didn't have time for his own family. Yet he had
promised William Riley. In a daze, Billy headed to Minneapolis to become the youngest college president in America.
He was twenty-nine.

Like every job he did, he threw tremendous energy into it.
Professors were taken aback by his calling them "gang," but he
forged ahead with no less a goal than making Northwestern
another Wheaton College! And he leaned on Grady Wilson's
brother, T. W., to take over as administrator. T. W. refused.
Billy harangued T. W. as persistently as William Riley had
harangued him. He phoned him eight days in a row. Finally,
T. W. took the position. Almost everyone at Northwestern

thought T. W. was as unsuited for administrator as Billy was for president.

When Ruth was asked when she would occupy the president's residence in Minneapolis, she snapped, "Never!"

With T. W. installed, Billy became an absentee president. He refused any salary and went on with his evangelizing. He wasn't about to get sidetracked. He would return to Minneapolis often enough to see that the Northwestern Bible Schools flourished, but he had more trips planned for England. And the chemistry of the new team he had assembled for the Charlotte crusade excited him. Split between the Bible school, his family at Montreat, and Youth for Christ, Billy knew 1948 was going to be hectic.

In Montreat, he bought a house across the street from Ruth's parents. It was obvious she could no longer cope in one upstairs bedroom of the Bell home. In May another daughter was born: Anne. And GiGi was proving to be unusually independent and spirited. On occasional trips to Charlotte, Ruth learned no one better understood a child who never ran out of energy than Billy's parents.

"Billy Frank just never ran down," said Billy's mother.

World events buttressed Billy's sermons on the evils of Communism. The Russians no longer hid their intentions. After the war, Berlin, which was an island inside Communist East Germany, had been partitioned into four parts. They were occupied by France, Britain, America, and Russia. The Russians blockaded all commerce from free West Germany, trying to starve the other occupying powers out of Berlin. But the three allies foiled the crude attempt by flying in supplies at a rate no one could have imagined.

In late 1948, Billy attended the formation of the World Council of Churches in Amsterdam. The organization espoused an ecumenical spirit that Billy approved of but a liberal theology that he could not accept. But his being there was in character. Billy would not condemn fellow Christians. He did not even condemn Communists. He loved people. But he would resist their mistaken ideas.

As Billy drew away from Northwestern more and more, he realized he wanted to evangelize away from the Youth for Christ organization, too. He wanted to evangelize everyone. He had great persuasion with youth. Somehow he could mellow the most rebellious young people with one or two corny jokes. It was a remarkable gift, because Billy wasn't funny. It was his unfunny way of telling a joke that was funny, and somehow it endeared him to listeners. But now Billy wanted to offer older people salvation, too. Or did he? He had made six trips across the Atlantic and campaigned in many American cities. Was he burning out?

"Or is it the influence of Chuck Templeton?" Billy grumbled to himself.

Charismatic Chuck Templeton was giving up evangelizing altogether. He had been accepted at Princeton Theological Seminary. He seemed to revile evangelizing now. He tried to pull Billy away, telling him he had stopped growing intellectually and his pulpit theology was literal and simple-minded. Billy respected Chuck Templeton very much, and he was confused by Templeton's new rationalism. He couldn't answer Templeton's erudite criticisms of the Bible. At times he was really tempted to join Templeton at Princeton.

Templeton kept saying, "You are committing intellectual suicide."

In November 1948, somewhat shaken by Templeton's defection, he called his closest friends together: Cliff Barrows, Bev Shea, and Grady Wilson. The team was evangelizing in Modesto, California. Harry Truman had kept the White House by upsetting Republican Thomas Dewey in the presidential election, but Billy had scarcely noticed.

"Gang," said Billy, gnawing on a fingernail, "we are on the brink of something bigger, I think. But we can't stop improving. Let's all go to our rooms and list all the things that are *wrong* with evangelism. Then we'll get together and discuss our lists and what to do about them."

So they tried to list their own flaws. When they compared lists, it was surprising how similar their lists were. One problem was the loose way they handled money. There must be no suspicion that they were lining their own pockets. They decided all offerings must be handled by a committee of the local clergy who invited them. The next problem was sexual temptation. They resolved with much prayer to avoid *all* situations that would put them alone with a woman, even something as innocent as a ride to the airport. The next problem was the common perception that they exaggerated their crowds. In the future, they would take police estimates even though they tended to be on the low side. Another problem was the perception that they exaggerated the number who came to the altar. They would admit right up front many of those coming to the altar were volunteers who were supposed to counsel the converts. They must study the cards the converts filled out and release accurate numbers. In fact, those who came to the altar were really not all converts. Some were just curious. Billy and his team would no longer call them converts. In the future they would call them "inquirers." Another problem was that evangelists in the past attacked the local clergy. They would guard against undermining authority of local pastors.

Thus armed with this "Modesto Manifesto," the team continued its evangelizing. They had great successes and a few failures, too. Sometimes the failure was in traveling. Once in Canada, Billy almost died in a plane landing in a blizzard. That very same night, he was mistakenly identified as a fugitive and arrested. A few incidents like that almost soured Billy on traveling. And he continued to talk to Chuck Templeton, who sank deeper into liberal theology every day. His doubts about anything being true in the Bible shook Billy. If the resurrection wasn't true, then they were to be pitied more than all men, thought Billy, just as the apostle Paul said in First Corinthians. Then Billy would remember Paul saying further:

Dear brothers, stand firm. Let nothing move you. Always give yourselves fully to the work of the Lord, because you know that your labor in the Lord is not in vain.

How could he doubt the Bible? Such doubt destroyed faith. But in late spring 1949, the city of Altoona brought him to his knees. Advance preparation had been haphazard because local clergy were fighting among themselves. The team went anyway. Turnouts were sparse. And some of those few who turned out seemed straight from an asylum. One woman stood up and threatened to kill Cliff Barrows, then rushed the pulpit. Grady Wilson and two ushers intercepted her. Billy sank into one of his black moments. Perhaps Chuck Templeton was right. Was this any kind of life? He was thirty now, past the blush of youth. Ruth was ever more distant. The children were strangers. Could Billy keep on? Should he keep on?

"Is my theology outdated, intellectually shallow?" he kept asking himself. "Are parts of the Bible not true?"

Somehow he bounced back and continued. But depression and doubts returned more and more. He got splitting headaches. His biggest campaign ever was on the horizon: Los Angeles in September 1949. How could he possibly pull himself together? His doubts made the advance work for Los Angeles dwarf the advance work done for Charlotte. He just couldn't fail in Los Angeles.

One month before the campaign was to begin, he was driving with Grady Wilson across Utah to the San Bernardino Mountains for a conference. Suddenly, he was overwhelmed with doubt. Why was it that he could not answer Chuck Templeton's questions about the Bible? Templeton must be right. Rationalism was true! Tears poured down his cheeks.

Grady was staring at him. "What's the matter, buddy?"

"Templeton said I am committing intellectual suicide. Maybe he's right."

"Pull over on that jeep trail," barked Grady.

A few minutes later, he and Grady were on their knees in the scrubby desert, praying out loud, beseeching God for help. They prayed on and on, shedding their shirts in the late summer heat. How many hours had he prayed over the years? Thousands! He remembered Olford's "quiet time." Faith had to be nurtured. Billy gradually felt his old confidence return as they prayed.

Two hours later, Billy rose. "Let's go!" he snapped, rejuvenated. Surely his faith was rock solid now.

But at the conference center called Forest Home, his faith failed again. Chuck Templeton was at the conference. Templeton and his liberal theologians stumped Billy. Their attacks on the Bible were so dazzling, he couldn't argue with them. Billy didn't read Greek. He couldn't pick passages apart and say a certain passage is not authentic, because the phraseology is such and so. And he couldn't argue with the weird psychology that a certain passage is authentic, because surely no one would embarrass themselves intentionally with such self-condemnation. And he couldn't dispute someone who claimed a certain passage is not authentic because pagans believed the same thing several hundred years earlier. Once again, liberal theologians had befuddled him, even soured him.

That night he stumbled into the forest in doubt, as he had once roamed the golf course at Florida Bible Institute in doubt. He prayed and prayed. Finally, it dawned on him that the critics of the Bible didn't apply the same rigor to the secular world. Few people knew how planes stayed in the air. Few knew the machinations of a car. How did a brown cow eat green grass and produce white milk? Did anyone care? No, they accepted it on faith. They were playing some kind of precocious child's game with the Holy Bible. They were hypocrites. They were to be pitied. He would pray for them.

And how could he have forgotten that the Lord quoted Scripture again and again? Billy almost let himself get slick-talked out of God's greatest gift to man, the gospel. He placed his Bible on a stump and knelt. "Oh God, I cannot prove certain things. I cannot answer some of the questions Chuck is raising and some of the other people are raising, but I accept this book by faith as the Word of God."[1] He rose. "From this moment on, I surrender myself to God's hands, heart, and soul."

Now maybe he was ready for his biggest test yet. . . .

The year 1949 was a strange one for Los Angeles. In January it snowed heavily; the downtown area recorded the coldest temperature in its history: 28 degrees Fahrenheit. Even in September, when the air should have been warm and dry, it was not. The air was cool and rainy. It made the extreme preparation for Billy's Greater Los Angeles Revival seem brilliant in hindsight. For three weeks the crusaders hoped to pack six thousand people six nights a week and twice on Sunday into Billy's "Canvas Cathedral"—a three-spired Ringling Brothers Circus tent—downtown on the corner of Washington and Hill streets. Armin Gesswein and Edwin Orr had labored mightily for nine months. They had organized eight hundred prayer groups to pray for the success of the revival. Dawson Trotman trained counselors to assist those who were to come to the altar. Cliff Barrows recruited a top-notch choir and singing groups.

Yet, Billy felt compelled to saturate Los Angeles with advertising, too. "I think we need to spend twenty-five thousand dollars," he said with utmost sincerity. "Consider it mustard seed. Over three weeks we hope to speak to one hundred thousand people."

Dazed, eyebrows raised, the local committee of Greater Los Angeles for Christ approved his request. They had invited other revivalists in past years, including Chuck Templeton. But never had any of their guest evangelists been so aggressive—and so expensive.

The campaign had the support of over 250 local churches as well as the mayor. Local celebrities were recruited, including Stuart Hamblen, a talented singing Texan with a daily radio program called *Cowboy Church of the Air*, but also with a reputation for living the good life. He was a drinking buddy of Hollywood movie stars like John Wayne.

When Billy went on Hamblen's show before the revival started, he was surprised to hear Hamblen blurt, "I'm going to be there, too!"

Most important to Billy's sense that all would go well was the rest of the team: Grady Wilson, Cliff Barrows, and Bev Shea. Grady was Billy's sidekick and jack-of-all-trades. He could organize prayer groups, preach if Billy got sick, tell funny stories, or cook breakfast. White-suited, halfback-burly Cliff, swinging his trombone, bounced through the singing like a cheerleader. Balancing Cliff or a local singing group was baleful dark-suited Bev Shea, who sang two hymns in somber reverence. Dignified Bev always preceded Billy's sermon to set the right tone. Since they had embraced a greater audience than youth only, Billy had toned down the service so that it was more a church service than a loud, colorful show.

His gaudy clothing was gone. He tended to wear dark suits more often, always with a handkerchief blossoming from the breast pocket. Billy started with a passage from the black Bible he clutched. "The Bible says. . . ," he would bellow, borrowing an old evangelist's phrase, before he went on to quote Scripture. Then began his ringing denunciation of those who disobeyed God's Word and the dreaded consequences. He wore a lapel microphone now, so he could be heard in the farthest corners. He still stalked the platform, cracking out honeyed southern words like pops of lightning. He locked his eyes on several hundred people at once. When he had them squirming, it was time for a change of pace. He would soften his tone for a while or move on to lambaste another segment of his audience. Billy hammered through the list of sins: materialism, alcoholism, adultery, suicide, stealing, cheating, divorce, greed. But he never forgot to be current. That is what it took to convince many skeptics that the Bible was relevant, even though new evils plagued man: rationalism, godless Communism.

And if any sinner assumed the dark suit had mellowed Billy into a detached saint, he was wrong. Stuart Hamblen quickly found that out. During the second week, Billy pistoled his finger in Hamblen's direction and snapped, "There's a man in here leading a double life!" The next night he leveled his finger at Hamblen again, "There's a phony in here tonight!" After that night, Hamblen refused to attend.

After three weeks it was customary to extend the crusade in Los Angeles if success merited it. Billy's success had been marginal. And the novelty was wearing off. The crowds were beginning to thin. Except for the greater expense he extracted from his hosts, he had enjoyed no more distinction than previous revivalists. But it was by no means a flop either, and the local committee asked him to decide himself if he wanted to extend the crusade. Billy had never extended a crusade before, no matter how successful, so to some on the team the gesture from their hosts was rather hollow.

"I'll put out a fleece," Billy said somewhat nervously Saturday, just one day before their last scheduled service. He was alluding to the story of Gideon in the book of Judges. One night Gideon put out a fleece on the threshing floor and asked God to give him a sign. If in the morning the fleece was covered with dew, yet the floor around it was completely dry, that would be a sign from God.

"But what is your fleece, Billy?" asked one of his contingent.

"It has been unseasonably cold or rainy ever since we got here. We'll see if the weather changes."

The weather had been cool every day. Billy's gesture, too, seemed hollow. Yet on Sunday, the air was uncomfortably warm inside the tent. Billy announced the revival would continue. After the first service of their extended campaign, in the middle of the night, Billy got a phone call from Stuart Hamblen. He was drunk and in complete turmoil over Billy's condemnation. He wanted to repent. Billy told him repentance in a drunken stupor meant nothing. But Hamblen came stumbling to Billy's room, and Billy prayed with Hamblen through the night. He wasn't too drunk to negotiate. Like the rich young ruler, he was loath to give up everything. Billy would not negotiate. Give up everything and repent—or stop wasting everyone's time, he told Hamblen. Hamblen caved in. Yes, he would give up everything. When he sobered, his new resolve remained. But Billy had seen hangover remorse before.

"Please, Lord, make Stuart's conversion stick," he prayed.

That same day Hamblen announced his repentance on his radio program, promising to give up alcohol, cigarettes, even all but one of his racehorses. He sheepishly explained he had to keep El Lobo—but he wouldn't race him. His wife and parents and friends were very skeptical. But he did amazing things, like denounce the very brand of cigarettes that sponsored his program. He refused to do beer commercials. After several days of sobriety, touting his repentance under the influence of Billy Graham, the conversion seemed real.

"I knew when I got him to eat grits that morning, the conversion was real," joked Grady.

Not long after that success, Billy called Louis Zamperini to the altar. In the 1930s, Zamperini had been a world-class distance runner, widely publicized for tearing down one of Hitler's swastikas at the 1936 Olympics. During the war as a combatant, he was adrift in a life raft for a month and a half in the Pacific. Then he survived a Japanese concentration camp. But eventually his great courage failed him. Until the Lord saved him under Billy's preaching, he found his courage in a liquor bottle.

Success snowballed. Not long after Zamperini testified on the platform, another man came to the altar. Billy learned this guilt-haunted man was drawn to the revival by the publicity over Stuart Hamblen. Of course the man didn't really believe Billy could save him, but he thought it wouldn't hurt to try. And the man came to the altar, reborn. He was Jim Vaux, a henchman for the czar of the Los Angeles underworld, Mickey Cohen. Billy even met secretly with Cohen himself, who was curious about the power of this hawk-eyed evangelist. Their meeting was leaked to the press, probably by Cohen himself, who loved publicity.

"You've been used," commented one of Billy's friends.

"We may need a larger tent," replied Billy, gnawing his fingernails. "I need to call Armin Gesswein. This is getting awfully big awfully fast now."

Celebrities like Gene Autry and Jane Russell began to attend the revival. Suddenly, the crusade was being touted in two Los Angeles newspapers, the *Herald* and the *Examiner*, with full-page stories and photos of Billy haranguing the crowd like John the Baptist. Both Los Angeles newspapers were owned by the old friend of the Youth for Christ: William Randolph Hearst. It only became apparent to the revivalists in Los Angeles that Hearst was running the story in his papers across the rest of the country when reporters from the national magazines *Life*, *Quick*, *Newsweek*, and *Time* showed up.

"Say, that's wonderful," gushed Billy.

But inside he was disconcerted because he was running out of sermons. Ruth was with him now. She had come in the third week, leaving GiGi with her parents and Anne with her sister, Rosa. She had planned to leave Los Angeles with Billy at the end of the week. Now she stayed through the extension, helping him every way she could. When she wasn't frantically outlining sermons, she pointed out the revival was now running on the Associated Press, United Press, and International News Service.

Billy was exhausted. He had delivered over sixty sermons. But fatigue was a tool of the devil. "The more tired I become physically, the stronger I must become spiritually," he declared, echoing the apostle Paul.

Hollywood gossip columnist Louella Parsons interviewed Billy and wrote a saccharine column. Billy felt like he could almost always win someone over one-on-one. It wasn't his charisma, he insisted. It was the power of the Holy Spirit. Cecil B. DeMille, the producer of quality biblical films like *Samson and Delilah*, offered him a screen test.

The Canvas Cathedral overflowed on his last meeting, November 20. The seating inside had been expanded to nine thousand. The crowd overflowed into the street as it had several times recently, blocking traffic. In eight weeks, Billy had drawn 350,000 listeners, of which 3,000 had come to the altar to inquire. Local churches helping him had swollen to seven hundred. Everything seemed magnified. One cleric suggested Billy start a church in Los Angeles. Billy was appalled.

"It will be kind of nice to get away from all the hubbub for a while," said Billy to Ruth as they boarded the train to Minneapolis the next day.

But the train was no refuge. Everyone seemed to know him now. The conductor and porters treated him like a celebrity. It was embarrassing being treated with so much respect when one had done nothing directly to them to earn it. At Kansas City, reporters rushed inside the train, asking questions and popping flashbulbs. He wanted to tell them to back off, but wouldn't he be betraying his friends? Wasn't this publicity what the revival movement needed?

In Minneapolis, as Billy addressed his amazed cohorts at Northwestern Bible School, he was suddenly overwhelmed by what happened in Los Angeles. He couldn't continue. He had to sit down, struck speechless.

EIGHT

It was more than the immensity of events catching up with Billy that robbed him of his tongue. He was run down. His doctor ordered him to rest one month.

"And rest I will," he agreed thankfully.

At Montreat, he played with four-year-old GiGi and eighteen-month-old Anne. And when the children tired him, the grandparents kept them across the street while Billy and Ruth had "quiet time." Once in a while, the success at Los Angeles would bubble up from his memory and overwhelm him. There was only one way to put Los Angeles in its proper perspective. Billy prayed and prayed, praising God for the power of the Holy Spirit. Billy was a mere instrument of God's will. He must never forget that.

"I know you're recovering now," commented Ruth one day.

"How do you know?" asked Billy.

"You're biting your fingernails, probably worrying about your next campaign."

"Boston?" said Billy breezily, but he was very worried.

Billy's team could not have picked a tougher city to evangelize. Boston was dominated by Catholics, and its Protestant clergy were so stodgy, they had refused to sponsor a Youth for Christ rally that Billy had tried to hold there once. The initial reaction of the New England Evangelical Association to Billy's latest proposal for a revival was to have Billy come for one sermon on New Year's Eve! More adventurous clergy had prevailed. Billy was scheduled for ten days. There had been little advance work. Everyone had been too busy with Los Angeles.

"The Boston venture is beginning to look like another Altoona," Billy told himself.

He opened the campaign with a press conference. The reporters were cynical. It was obvious they thought Billy was a fast-buck artist. Finally, he pulled a telegram out his pocket. "I've turned this offer down. Do you still think I'm after money?" The telegram from Hollywood described an offer to pay Billy over two hundred thousand dollars to star in two movies!

The initial stories from the five Boston newspapers were respectful. Maybe Billy wasn't a con artist after all. The first night Billy preached to six thousand at Mechanics Hall. When he invited them to the altar, his team held its breath.

"One hundred and seventy-five," said their host, Harold Ockenga, slightly dazed. "In Boston?"

Enthused at such success, they announced an impromptu meeting the next afternoon. The only other notice of the meeting was in a few hastily amended Sunday morning church bulletins. Nevertheless, Billy preached to another six thousand with the same success. At the regularly scheduled meeting that night, two thousand had to be turned away. The next night they turned away seven thousand!

The response was stunning. There had been no advance work to speak of. Mindful of how success could corrupt, Billy invited his hosts to prayer. He beseeched them, "Pray that the Lord will remind me that this is His Glory! I must not take the tiniest bit of credit. Or His hand will leave me." Deep inside, Billy felt his hosts, once so skeptical that he was just a slick operator, were startled by his closeness to God.

His Feast of Belshazzar sermon was standard now. It was Billy's metaphor for modern man's pride and separation from God. But now he delivered it in American slang:

> [Belshazzar bragged] I'm going to put on the biggest
> shindig in Babylon. . .[Belshazzar] was one of those
> smart fellows who think they can do as they please and
> forget all about God. But, brother, that's where he was
> wrong. . . . It makes no difference if you are the king of
> Babylon or the president, or anybody important. You
> are no exception to the law of God. . . . He doesn't
> care. . .whether you came over on the Mayflower. . . .

"Good grief," muttered one of the local clergy. "That common touch will never work here in Boston."

Billy launched into Daniel's fate in the lions' den:

> Old Daniel walks in. He's not afraid. He looks the first
> big cat in the eye and kicks him and says, "Move over
> there, Leo. I want me a nice fat lion with a soft belly
> for a pillow, so I can get a good night's rest. . . ."[1]

91

"Ugh, that's even homelier," said the cleric.

Bostonians flocked to the altar.

The Boston rallies grew. Billy was invited to open the state legislature with a prayer. Shifting from auditorium to auditorium now to accommodate the much larger than expected crowds, Billy finally found himself in his final meeting at Boston Garden, where the Celtics played basketball. The revivalists jammed sixteen thousand inside, with another ten thousand standing outside. Bostonians were singing hymns in the street. Billy was scared, his successes were becoming so enormous. In a way, he could understand Los Angeles. Boston was beyond understanding. His preaching had never been better though; he knew that. The crowds were inspiring him to new heights. Yet he reminded himself constantly that he was speaking through the Holy Spirit. He must not take credit. He really believed if he did, his power would end as suddenly as it did for Moses when he struck the rock at Kadesh.

On the train away from Boston, he told Ruth, "It seems like my heart is crying out to me to go back. The finale at Boston Garden was a sign that we were on the verge of some colossal new awakening. Folks were singing in the streets. There was great joy."

"Why can't we go back?"

"Too much on our schedule." But he had an ache in his heart as if he would regret not going back as long as he lived. Had he disobeyed God?

And he ruminated over the press. He would have to be more careful with reporters. He felt so euphoric after a successful meeting. And they peppered him with questions. He just felt like he could answer anything.

Ruth showed him the newspaper. "Did you say heaven was 1,600 miles wide, 1,600 miles high and 1,600 miles deep?"

"Did they report that?"

"Yes, with walls of jasper, streets of gold, and gates of pearl."

"Revelation 21."

"And will we drive down the golden streets in a yellow Cadillac?"

He would have to stop spouting off after meetings about what heaven would be like and such things that were vague in the Bible. He would have to stick closer to God's true Word than ever. And he would have to be more careful about his comments on Communists inside America. There was a swelling undercurrent of vigilante justice that he didn't like.

"Did you say you wanted President Truman's ear for thirty minutes?" asked Ruth.

"Wouldn't that help spread the gospel?" he replied defensively, gnawing on a fingernail. But it was a good thing he hadn't told the reporter he had sent the president a telegram asking for a meeting.

He preached for three weeks in Columbia, South Carolina. Willis Haymaker had done the advance work. His work was masterful. He organized prayer groups, which was standard operating procedure, but he seemed to do it better than anyone else had before. He also got local churches to block out certain nights so every meeting had the core of a good audience. Haymaker was the first to call the revivals a "crusade" to imply it was an ongoing effort that would not end when Billy left town. Haymaker was an innovator. Billy had never seen such thorough work. Billy also added Tedd

Smith, a classical pianist, to help Cliff. The South Carolina rally was a model crusade.

The governor of South Carolina, Strom Thurmond, backed Billy. Billy went to the state legislature as he had done in Boston. But this time he gave a speech warning America not to backslide as the Jews did in the time of Isaiah. The circus tent and sawdust were long gone. His crusade was a success, and again he could not believe the opportunities that came to him. At the governor's mansion, he met one of the most influential men in America: Henry Luce.

Luce owned *Time* and *Life*. But opportunity does not always result in success. Under shaggy eyebrows, Henry Luce watched Billy with eyes as penetrating as Billy's own. Luce was boldly assessing him: Was Billy a phony or not? After two nights of talking, Luce's eyes glowed. A team from *Life* was rushed to South Carolina for the final meetings.

"The last meeting of the crusade is where?" Billy asked his hosts incredulously.

"University of South Carolina football stadium," answered his hosts. "It holds thirty-five thousand."

Billy was aghast. "Can we fill it?"

"Oh, you of little faith," cracked one of the contingent.

Billy had to laugh. He had used that very quote to win an argument a few days earlier. But why take such a chance? Did they have to push God to the limit? This success wasn't Billy's doing. Hadn't God done enough for one crusade? But it was too late. The stadium was news already. And *Life* would be there to report on its huge pages Billy's glaring success or failure.

"What if it rains? Did you think about that?" Billy wanted to ask his hosts, but he attacked a fingernail instead.

All the while Billy strode to the platform for the finale, he praised God. Forty thousand people crowded inside the football stadium. Ten thousand were turned away. Billy preached about Noah and the flood as God's judgment. And there was a great flood of people who came to the altar. It was another colossal success. How could he top that?

But his acceptance by Henry Luce and the South Carolina governor's mansion spread like wildfire to the highest circles in the country. Billy was invited to pray before the United States Congress in Washington, D.C. There he was praised by the Speaker of the House, Sam Rayburn. Billy was more and more nervous about success. It was all too much, too fast. When would he falter? He had to remind himself that Billy Graham wasn't going to succeed or falter. His success was God's success. But the reporters kept turning it into Billy Graham's success. And he had to keep repeating, "No, no; this is God's glory."

He returned to New England. In spite of his worry over such success, he felt he had to seize the moment and be bold. To a crowd estimated at fifty thousand by the Boston police, he urged President Truman to call for a day of national repentance as President Lincoln had done. And Billy outlined his own five-point plan for peace. The first three points were to maintain security through military, internal, and economic strengths. The fourth was to put aside all divisiveness and unite all races and creeds. His fifth was to have a moral and spiritual regeneration through repentance and faith in Christ.

No one could doubt Billy had risen to prominence when he received an invitation after the New England crusade.

Billy was stunned. "Grady, what do we have scheduled for July 14?"

"Let me see. . . ."

"Never mind. Cancel it. We've been invited to the White House."

Grady was giddy. "The White House? President Truman?"

"That's right," said Billy. "July 14."

"How should we dress?"

"What do you mean?" asked Billy. "Wear a dark suit and black shoes."

"But Truman is a casual guy. Haven't you seen pictures of him at Key West in his spiffy white bucks and loud Hawaiian shirts?"

"We can't wear Hawaiian shirts to the White House," argued Billy.

"What about white bucks?"

That seemed like a great idea. That would definitely break the ice. Billy enthused, "We could wear light summer suits, handpainted ties, and white bucks. Let the president know we're down-to-earth folks—just like he is."

And that's how Billy, Cliff Barrows, Grady Wilson, and Jerry Beaven, the newest member of the team, dressed for the meeting at the White House with the single most powerful man in the world. They showed up well ahead of time and sat outside the Oval Office, squirming. Watchless, Billy asked his friends what time it was every few seconds.

Finally, they were taken into the office.

The bespectacled president greeted them, adding good-naturedly that he was a Baptist. Truman stood ramrod straight in a dark suit. As Billy began to preach for a national day of repentance, the president interrupted him impatiently. "I live by the Sermon on the Mount and the Golden Rule. I said I was a Baptist. . . ."

Perhaps Billy could get his message about what America needed to do in Korea into a prayer. "Would it be all right if we prayed before we leave, Mr. President?"

"I don't suppose it could do much harm."

Billy put his arm around the president and delivered his message in prayer, as Cliff chanted, "Yes, do it, Lord," and, "Amen." The four were besieged by reporters as they left the White House. Billy told them what he had said. But when the reporters asked him to go out on the front lawn of the White House and kneel in prayer as he had done in the meeting, he objected. First of all, they hadn't knelt in prayer. Secondly, simulating prayer was wrong. But finally one enterprising reporter asked him to kneel on the lawn and actually give a prayer of thanks for meeting with the president. This Billy agreed to do.

Billy was very pleased with his meeting.

"Drew Pearson's column in the newspaper says we really goofed," said one of his team to Billy later. "Says we shouldn't have talked about what was said in the meeting and that the president is real mad about it."

"Oh Lord, how puffed up we were," said Billy, remembering. "Pride. That's what did us in."

" 'My son, do not despise the LORD's discipline and do not resent his rebuke,' " said Ruth. "Isn't that one of your favorite verses?" she added not so innocently.

"Proverbs 3:11," confirmed Billy. "Amen. God yanked us up short and booted us right in the seats of our white pants!"

Billy certainly had no right to complain. They were prideful that day at the White House. Besides, his one-on-one meetings were almost always successful. Surely he couldn't expect to be successful every time. He moved on to his Portland crusade. Things were happening at a feverish pace. Two friends of his ministry, Walter Bennett and Fred Dienert, were trying to negotiate a package for a weekly radio program with the ABC network. At first Billy was enthused. But when he realized the program would cost his organization seven thousand dollars a week, besides costing him hours and hours of precious time to prepare a flawless program, he balked. When the two men told him ABC wanted thirteen weeks guaranteed, or ninety-two thousand dollars, Billy almost fainted.

"The answer is no," he said. And now he avoided the two negotiators.

He had become more and more a captive of his popularity. It was difficult to walk about freely now. He spent more and more time in his hotel room when he was not preaching—like he did now in the Multnomah Hotel in Portland. Often he would still be in his room at noon, eating lunch delivered by room service, in his pajamas, and wearing a green baseball cap to keep his unruly hair matted down. Then before he finally left to preach, he would eat a light meal with tea.

The crusade in Portland was another staggering success. Each one seemed to get larger. In Portland, the block-square tabernacle of aluminum and wood held twelve thousand seats. Standing-room-only crowds reached twenty thousand. In six weeks he had preached to half a million people. They tried a "Ladies Only" meeting, which turned into a melee. Thirty thousand women showed up, tearing down traffic barriers and climbing over automobiles.

In the meantime, Bennett and Dienert pestered Billy like

the persistent widow. Now they insisted he needed only twenty-five thousand dollars up front. Finally, he threw out the fleece. He would have been appalled if someone said he only did that when he wanted to kill a project, but when he announced the terms of this "fleece," it did seem that way.

"If the Lord wants me to do this, I will have the twenty-five thousand dollars tonight—before midnight."

Not all his followers were aghast. One calculated, "If we draw twenty thousand people tonight, and Billy tells them about the radio opportunity before the love offering, I think he'll get it for sure."

But even that optimist was aghast that night at the rally. Billy did not tell his audience about the radio opportunity *before* the love offering; he told them *after* the offering. And he told them in a low-key, almost halfhearted way that the radio program would require twenty-five thousand dollars and that if anyone wanted to encourage this kind of evangelizing, they could donate money after the service.

"Well, we can bury that idea," grumbled a follower.

Unbelievably, people lined up afterward, coming one by one to the table where Billy was sitting with Grady Wilson. Money poured into a shoebox: five dollars, loose change, twenty dollars, and an occasional lunker like a check for twenty-five hundred dollars. Billy sat there, completely trusting God, saying over and over, "God bless you. Thank you."

After the line was exhausted, Billy didn't count the money. He gave the shoebox to their host committee and left to eat a late supper. It was during the meal that the team learned they had raised 23,500.

"It's a miracle!" screamed one of the diners.

"It's not enough," said Billy. "The devil is tempting us."

They trudged back to the hotel. They picked up their mail at the desk and rode the elevator up to their rooms. Billy felt sick. He couldn't have made the test any harder. Still, the fleece was plain enough. God had spoken. Inside Billy's room, Grady sorted through the mail.

"Say!" blurted Grady. "This envelope has a pledge in it for the radio program. Somebody must have dropped it off at the desk after the meeting broke up. Two hundred and fifty bucks. . ."

Now all eyes were on the stack of mail.

Sweat popped out on Grady's forehead as he opened letter after letter. He was smiling all the while he read the letters out loud. A check fluttered out of one envelope onto the table. Grady's smile almost split his face. "Another check for the radio program. One thousand dollars."

"How much is that then? Anybody totaled it all up?" asked Cliff Barrows.

"Twenty-four thousand seven hundred and fifty," said Grady, now grumpy as he realized it was not enough. He pawed through the rest of the mail, opening letter after letter. Then he pulled a check from one letter and smiled.

"Bingo. Two hundred and fifty dollars." The total had reached exactly twenty-five thousand dollars!

Billy wanted to call the radio program *Deciding for Christ*, but Ruth volunteered *Hour of Decision*. The team preferred Ruth's name. *Hour of Decision* went on the air November 5, 1950, over 150 ABC stations. The first broadcast was from an actual revival in Atlanta.

After Atlanta, the *Hour of Decision* would typically open

with the stirring "Battle Hymn of the Republic," followed by Cliff Barrows's introduction, which ended with "This is the *Hour of Decision!*"

Then came Grady Wilson reading a passage from the Bible. Jerry Beaven would read the news. Bev Shea would sing a hymn to set a somber, respectful mood. Then came what everyone waited for: Billy Graham. Billy would start with a development in the news, breathlessly, dramatically, like famed radio personalities Walter Winchell and Drew Pearson. The resemblance ended there. Billy brought in the Bible and relentlessly hammered his audience, never faltering for a word. The listener got no relief from Billy's impending hell without Christ until he said, "Goodnight and may the Lord bless you," then drawled a honeyed, "real good."

The crusade in Atlanta also had another memorable event for Billy. He met the widow of the great evangelist Billy Sunday. And Ma Sunday, as she was called, had some bitter advice.

NINE

B oys," said Ma Sunday, "I know you have to travel night and
day to spread the gospel. It's the Great Commission. But
don't let your wives neglect your children. I thought I had to
travel all over the country with Billy Sunday. We unknowingly
sacrificed our own children." Tears streamed down her face. "All
four went straight to hell."

Billy had heard of the tragedy of Billy Sunday's children.
He had felt very guilty about Ruth staying behind in North
Carolina with GiGi and Anne. Ruth was seven months' pregnant at that very moment. He would try never to feel guilty
again. He would miss his children. He would feel sad but
never guilty.

The money situation was getting complicated. Billy had to
be incorporated now that so much money was pouring in. It
was crucial he stay clear of any suspicion of money-grubbing.
He objected to calling his organization the Billy Graham
Evangelical Association, but even Ruth insisted his name had

to be in the title. "What was he hiding?" she asked, mocking a reporter. And he was to be given the salary of a minister of a large church. No more and no less.

Within months, the number of radio stations carrying the *Hour of Decision* doubled. The Billy Graham Evangelical Association got larger and larger. With the commitments of weekly radio and never-ending citywide crusades, the demands were great. The BGEA, headquartered in Minneapolis, added people to write scripts and take care of a thousand details. Already Billy and his team were considering a television program and a weekly newspaper column. "And how about a book?" asked one eager follower, puzzled by the answering groans.

The organization began compiling a mailing list of sympathetic supporters. "BGEA won't use the list to hound folks for money," vowed Billy. But it didn't hurt to keep supporters informed of their opportunities and drop the gentlest reminder that evangelizing required money.

If 1950 wasn't momentous enough, Ruth gave birth to their third daughter on December 19. The infant was named Ruth Bell but almost immediately got nicknamed "Bunny." Now GiGi and Anne, aged five and two, had a real-live doll. Billy tried to get to Montreat whenever he could.

In 1951, Billy got talked into sponsoring Christian films. He formed World Wide Pictures, which made two movies called *Mr. Texas* and *Oiltown*. He even had a premiere for *Mr. Texas* in Hollywood with Cecil B. DeMille in the audience. In spite of stinging criticism of the film as hopelessly amateurish, Billy just shrugged and prayed their efforts would get better. He had no intention of abandoning this promising approach to spreading the gospel. And the "star" of *Mr. Texas* drove about the country showing his film to whoever was willing to watch.

Billy also launched a weekly television show called *Hour of Decision*. The show aired stirring clips of his crusades. Other times, the show had Billy sitting in a comfortable chair as if in a home library and delivering a calm, reasoned, low-key message. Sometimes he would give rehearsed responses to questions. He personally did not believe such a low-key approach was very effective, but maybe he could persuade some listeners who were turned off by the stronger approach of his personal appearances and his radio program. He had no intention of giving up the television show, either.

"I learned long ago to open many doors," he reminded himself.

Billy continued his citywide crusades. He had no thought about stopping, even if he was stretched very thin. Independent of Youth for Christ, he had preached for three years to several million people in many American cities. The crusades were maturing. Billy had stopped all love offerings. Now a man or a woman need bring nothing but their souls to the revival. That was where the BGEA was so convenient. His radio and television shows inspired money to pour in to the Minneapolis office, where it was all meticulously accounted for. Never again would Billy be embarrassed by a photograph showing his ministry carrying away what appeared to be bags of money after a crusade. Billy figured a several-week citywide crusade now required a quarter of a million dollars. But he had another iron-clad requirement. He had to be invited by a solid majority of local churches, who would wholeheartedly participate and offer volunteers.

But the crusades were far from perfected. They still needed

improvement. One great need was follow-up. Far too many times, many inquirers flooded to the altar, then waited in vain in a logjam for counseling. What were they supposed to do next? Finally, many walked away. Billy was a fisher of men who was letting his catches slide back into the sea. It took many appeals by Billy to get the best man in the country to train his counselors full-time. But finally, he got Dawson Trotman, founder of the Navigators, a group unsurpassed in counseling one-on-one and nurturing the Word in a new Christian.

Another need was gnawing at him. He had always called everyone to the altar together, even calling out pointedly, "The ground is level at the foot of the cross. I want all white folks, all colored folks to come forward." Yet he was still setting aside sections for blacks, thoughtfully placing them in the shade or trying to soften their segregation with some other minor convenience. Wasn't it time for that to end? How could he approve of any form of segregation? But what would happen to his ministry in the South? The Jim Crow laws were rigidly enforced.

"I must search the Scriptures," he said.

Billy wasn't searching for the right or wrong of segregation. He knew in his heart segregation was not in Christ. But he was pragmatic. The Bible cautioned one to be wise in the worldly ways of men. White folks had to be won over gradually. Billy wasn't a hypocrite. It was the same way he handled prejudice against himself. He never flew into someone because they criticized him or let him down. He approached them with love and friendly persuasion, and it helped a bit to show hurt feelings. Yes, he was committed to doing something about segregation, but it would be slow and cautious.

In his crusades, Billy now praised movers and shakers

who could be most instrumental in stopping Communism. One of the most revered was General "Ike" Eisenhower, the commander of all allied forces in Europe in the Second World War. Ike was so popular, he was being courted as a candidate for president in the 1952 election. The intriguing thing was that no one knew for sure if he was a Democrat or a Republican. He had never even said he wanted to run for president. Billy wrote Ike a letter assuring him millions of Americans wanted him as president in these dangerous times, so perhaps he was morally obligated to run. Billy wrote many other movers and shakers, too, always suggesting they get together for a "chat." He didn't always get his wish, but at least now he always received a response.

Billy mounted his crusade in Washington, D.C., in early 1952. He was still refining his BGEA and at last resigned from the Northwestern Bible Schools. He had served them four years, much longer than he promised William Riley. He had finally taken a small token salary but didn't feel good about that. It was time for them to get a full-time president. Everything was falling neatly in place for the Washington crusade except for one detail: President Truman. Billy had implored him to put his stamp of approval on the crusade by attending at least one meeting. He got a curt "no."

"God, forgive me," muttered Billy, "but I think we need a new president."

Billy was deluged with other politicians. One-third of the senators requested special reserved seating for the crusade, and so had one-fourth of the members of the House. The most powerful endorsement was from Speaker of the House Sam Rayburn.

Rayburn said, "This country needs a revival, and I believe Billy Graham is bringing it to us."[1]

One nod from Sam Rayburn, and Billy attained the impossible: He got to hold his final rally on the steps of the Capitol! Billy drew over three hundred thousand in five weeks. He met legendary people like Douglas MacArthur. He made many friends among politicians in both parties. Among them were Lyndon Johnson and Richard Nixon. Billy remembered meeting Nixon's parents on a crusade in California. Nixon's mother had been very concerned about Billy keeping his weight up.

Billy kept expanding his organization within America during 1952. In addition to his radio and television shows, he started a weekly newspaper column called "My Answer," in which he answered pressing modern problems with Scripture. The answers were not ghosted. He would dictate an answer, which would be polished by a professional writer. Then Billy had to give that polished answer one last review.

"I don't want my newspaper column to be above criticism," he said, "but I do want it to be above suspicion that it's phony."

There was serious talk of a book now. New York publisher Doubleday approached him. Naturally they wanted a bestseller. Billy wanted a down-to-earth explanation of the meaning of Christ, maybe like the popular book by C. S. Lewis, *Mere Christianity*, but in Billy's style, stressing a greater urgency to seek salvation. But how was Billy to go about it? In his wildest daydream, he couldn't write like Lewis. Doubleday suggested he send an outline and his sermons that he felt were relevant. Doubleday could get an editor to put it all together. So Billy worked on it.

His family kept growing. Franklin was born July 14, 1952.

The Grahams now had four children: GiGi, almost seven; Anne, four; Bunny, eighteen months; and infant Franklin. Ruth accompanied Billy less and less. Billy had purchased two hundred acres of wooded mountain behind their house, so unappreciated it cost a mere sixteen dollars an acre. But Ruth seemed very much interested in building a home in a more secluded setting. Tourists were starting to poke around, looking for the Graham residence on Assembly Drive.

In November, Eisenhower ran for president as a Republican and won the election. Even though Billy was not appreciated by Harry Truman, he did get off on the right foot with the new President-elect Eisenhower. Billy had given him a gift of a red Bible as far back as Ike's nomination. Ike seemed to really like Billy. He even picked Billy as his religious consultant for the inauguration in January.

"At least Ike will let me go visit the troops in Korea someday," Billy said to Ruth. He had tried to get permission for a trip to Korea, which was now a battleground just as he predicted. Communist North Korea had invaded South Korea. United Nations' forces led by America were helping South Koreans defend themselves. He added ruefully, "Truman let Cardinal Spellman go."

"And you can be thankful for that," answered Ruth.

Abruptly in December, the Truman administration allowed him to go. "Why let Ike get any credit?" they must have asked themselves. Billy would get there for Christmas. During the long flight to Korea, Ruth revealed how different her perspective on life was. The team had pulled practical jokes on each other for years. Besides the normal short-sheeting of beds and Alka Seltzer in ink bottles, they were prone to loading hats and shoes with shaving lather. Slapstick humor was a great release from constant pressure. But Ruth, the girl who had spent years learning boarding school pranks, the woman who would still put a dead snake in a sack and leave it on a friend's porch, topped them all.

It started when Grady bragged, "I got the perfect solution to long flights. See these little yellow sandmen?" He brandished a bottle of yellow sleeping capsules. "While you all squirm and ache and groan all the way to Korea, ole Grady is going to be zonked out."

Billy learned Ruth had made a slight change in Grady's master plan. Just before the flight, she emptied Grady's wonder capsules and filled them with mustard powder. Grady's dreamy dreamland became a long nightmare of retching in a sick bag and wondering how the rest of the team could laugh so heartlessly at a fellow traveler's misery.

Once in the theater of war, the team's welcome was unexpectedly warm. Mark Clark, the commanding general of all the forces, personally welcomed them. Billy was treated like a "V.I.P.," getting an entourage to escort him to the troops. But his joy soon ended. Unlike Ruth, he had never seen men mangled by war before. In the hospital, one soldier, totally helpless, face down in a contraption, begged to see Billy. Billy crawled underneath to lie on the floor and pray with him. By the time Billy visited the combat zone, he felt no urge to be a drummer leading the charge. He now knew what the soldiers knew. He wanted only to give them hope. And he prayed for the war to end.

On the way back to Montreat, he told Ruth, "I feel like I went to Korea a boy, and I'm coming back a man." And he admired her more than ever.

Billy went to Ike before the inauguration. Ike really did want to consult with him about religion. Ike wanted Scripture for his inauguration speech. Billy made suggestions, and Ike chose a passage from Second Chronicles. The press now talked about Billy in the same breath as the most famous evangelists in American history: Billy Sunday and Dwight Moody. Billy remembered how Sunday had reached out to black Americans when it was extremely unpopular to do so. Billy had to think about the race question again. The Korean experience had really sobered him. Black soldiers were dying right beside white soldiers. When was Billy going to insist segregation in America be stopped?

In March 1953, at his Chattanooga crusade, Billy could not deny the truth of the gospel any longer. He was angry when he saw ushers putting up ropes to separate blacks and whites. Why hadn't he noticed before? He strode back and ripped down the ropes himself. He announced publicly, "Jesus Christ belongs neither to the colored nor the white races. . . . There are no color lines with Christ, as He repeatedly said that God looks upon the heart."[2] But it had an ironic result. The turnout of blacks was about the poorest he ever had. They were uneasy sitting with whites. The irony was emphasized again later in Dallas, where Billy fought unsuccessfully to prevent segregated seating. Thousands of blacks attended. The answer to the race question was very complicated, indeed. He had to keep crusading in the South, while he fought tooth and nail for unsegregated seating. Hearts had to be changed.

In July 1953, Eisenhower stopped the fighting in Korea just as Billy prayed he would. The war in Korea had been a nightmare for Billy from its beginning. It wasn't that he thought

America shouldn't have been involved. He couldn't imagine a greater evil than godless Communism. No, it was the half-hearted use of the most powerful military force in the world that bothered him, the halfheartedness that cost two thousand American lives a week at one point. Thank God it was over.

"Take a look at this," said Ruth to Billy one day.

"Oh, no. I can hear the exasperation in your voice."

It was the manuscript back from Doubleday. The ghost-writer's superficial knowledge of the gospel had made a hodge-podge of the proposed book. So Billy threw the manuscript away and sat down with Ruth to write a new manuscript. Friends critiqued it, and they rewrote it again. It cost Billy a chunk of time, but he was very proud of the manuscript. Surely this was God's doing. The book was now truly his—and Ruth's. He mailed it to Doubleday. They agreed to publish it late in 1953 as *Peace with God*.

"Can't we coast for a while?" asked Ruth.

"I've been thinking. Do you remember what happened in England last year?"

"When you spoke at Westminster? Their British Council of Churches turned down your idea for a real crusade. They got cold feet and wanted you to try the provinces first."

"But I was also invited by the Evangelical Alliance."

"Oh heavens, are you going to go through with that? I felt most of the clerics even in the Evangelical Alliance were hostile to a crusade."

It was not like Billy to go where he wasn't wanted. In fact, it was a maxim for his crusades. Why had he decided that England qualified for a crusade? Was it the memory of his earlier triumphs with Youth for Christ? England had been wonderful then. Or was it the specter of Dwight Moody? Billy wasn't a mindless robot. He knew his history. Only one American evangelist ever created a sensation abroad: Dwight Moody. Moody had revivals all over Great Britain. It had been almost one hundred years ago, yet the revivals were so electrifying, they were still talked about among churchmen in Great Britain.

Billy decided to go. His prospects for a successful crusade in London were bolstered at home. Ike wished him well. Even Earl Warren of the Supreme Court lead a prayer to wish him well.

"But the disheartened England of 1954 is not the England that won the Second World War," worried Ruth.

Billy knew Ruth was probably expressing the sentiments of her father, Nelson Bell, who was very savvy about international politics. And then Billy started to worry, too. Why was he going to England? His citywide crusades in America were always successful now. And the only facility they could find in London was lackluster Harringay Arena, right by a dog racing track in north London, in a neighborhood so run down, many Londoners might be afraid to attend a crusade.

"You've got to go with me, Ruth," he said.

Ruth raised an eyebrow. "You really are worried, aren't you?"

Ruth soothed him enough to remember two key ingredients to a good crusade, prayer and publicity, were working for his success already. He had eighteen thousand faithful in England praying for the crusade. The crusade had launched an advertising campaign in London so aggressive that thirty thousand posters were distributed. They had spent a staggering sum for the time: fifty thousand English pounds.

A confident Billy sailed with Ruth for England on the *United States* in February. But before the ship ever docked in

England, he got word the British were up in arms over his frequent criticisms of Socialism, which he used almost interchangeably with Communism. Socialism was a respectable option in England. The Labour Party had governed for several years after the war, before conservative Winston Churchill became prime minister again. But more than that, cradle-to-grave Socialism was a sacred cow to the press. When the ship docked at Southampton and the team disembarked, a horde of twenty-five reporters and eleven photographers swarmed around them like angry hornets.

"If Jesus were alive today, would he wear a hundred-dollar suit?" scoffed one reporter.

Billy opened his coat to the label. "J. C. Penney," he read. He resisted asking the reporter how much his suit cost.

"Would Jesus travel on a luxury liner?" sneered another reporter.

Grady laughed. "If you can find a donkey that can swim the Atlantic Ocean, Billy will take it next time."

But the reporters were not mollified. Their questions dripped with sarcasm:

"Do you think you can save England?"

"Since our crime rate is much lower than yours in the United States, why are you here?"

"How much money do you plan to haul out of England?"

Billy and Ruth soon learned the reporters were not merely threatening him, swords drawn. The swords were thrust home. Reports in the London newspapers were uncompromisingly vicious. Even the photographs of Billy were snide, one captioned: NO CLERICAL COLLAR, BUT MY! WHAT A LOVELY TIE!

The unrelenting hostility crippled Billy. The day of the first meeting, he had one of his darkest moments. What was he doing here? He had violated his own maxim: Don't go where you are not wanted. He had gambled and lost. Even Ike's support wasn't enough to keep the American ambassador to England from withdrawing from him. He would not attend the first meeting or any meeting. That was how badly things were going with the crusade.

One of the team came to him in his hotel room not long before the meeting was supposed to start. "I just talked to folks at the arena, Billy."

"Great," said Billy, gnawing a fingernail, trying to keep his spirits high. "Are they turning people away yet?"

"A couple of thousand are there, Billy."

"It should be full by now," mumbled Billy. The arena held twelve thousand. Billy got up and stood by the window. "It's snowing."

"There are about two hundred reporters there." His informant laughed uneasily.

Billy sat down. "And Senators Symington and Bridges?" Surely they wouldn't withdraw from him, even though he heard the ambassador had discouraged them from attending.

"They're not there. . .yet. They have a dinner engagement or something. They'll probably just be late," the man added unconvincingly.

The ride to the arena was somber. Next to the arena, the dog track was lit up and thronging with patrons. But the parking lot to the arena was almost empty. Billy trudged dejectedly inside the arena.

TEN

Inside the arena, Billy had to blink his eyes. "It's packed to the rafters! Oh God, forgive me," he prayed, "for not trusting You. This is Your glory, not mine. How did they get here so suddenly? And where are the cars?"

"These are Londoners," answered one of his hosts. "They came on the underground. Last minute, old chap. Quite suddenly."

"There are Senator Symington and Senator Bridges," gasped Billy. "I thought they weren't coming."

"Their dinner engagement is after your meeting," explained someone.

In the first sermon, Billy jabbed the air. "There's a hunger for God in London!"

And he was right. Londoners flocked to the arena day after day. One great innovation was originated by Stephen Olford, the Welshman who had already greatly influenced Billy. It was dubbed "Operation Andrew," after the apostle who brought his brother Peter to Christ. The purpose was to get the unchurched to the crusade. Any churched member would get free transportation to the crusade—if he brought an unchurched person with him.

Billy was still mellowing. His delivery was slower. A stenographer could almost keep up with him. He didn't stalk the platform as energetically. Extra meetings had to be scheduled, sometimes three a day. Londoners hungered for God, he kept reminding himself, not for Billy Graham. But he could show them how to find God. The Church of England quickly came into the fold. Realizing not sponsoring Billy was a horrible blunder, they now offered their own clergy as counselors. And of course Billy gratefully welcomed their participation.

"Much more potential remains untapped," explained his hosts, who were now scrambling to maximize his message. "We're turning people away by the thousands."

So his ingenious hosts set up a network of sites, with Billy's sermon relayed to each site by telephone. Now each sermon was heard at over four hundred churches and rented halls in 175 cities in Great Britain and Ireland. At each site, the local clergy participated, talking to the audience before the sermon and counseling them afterward, just as they would have done at the arena.

Ruth was with him all the while. It was the longest she had ever been away from the children. At one point, she made a reservation to fly back, but Billy canceled it. He felt so strong when she was there, even though the two and three revivals a day were draining him. His wiry frame was losing what little weight it carried.

Later he thought about Ma Sunday and relented.

"Maybe you better go back, Ruth."

"No, I'm staying for the duration. I've thought it over. The children will certainly be all right with their grandparents this once."

At the London School of Economics, Billy spoke to students who had come to ridicule him. They booed him as he stood up. Billy told several corny jokes, which mysteriously calmed most of the students. His transparent sincerity had always defused bad intentions. But suddenly a student disrupted Billy by prancing and scratching like an ape.

"He reminds me of my ancestors," quipped Billy.

The students roared with laughter, sure the American evangelical had been caught conceding the truth of evolution.

Billy added, "Of course, all my ancestors came from Britain."[1]

By the end of twelve weeks, even the press fell under Billy's unrelenting sincerity and goodness. One columnist from the *Daily Express*, William Hickey, admitted he goaded Billy unmercifully during an interview but was suddenly overwhelmed by the realization:

*He is a good man. I am not sure he isn't a saintly man. . . .
But make no mistake about this. Billy Graham is a
remarkable man. . . . Perhaps he is what Britain needs. . . .
It is a bitter pill to swallow. . .[after Graham left me]
my eyes were scalding with tears.[2]*

One of his most vicious detractors was a columnist named William Conner, who wrote for the *Daily Mirror* as "Cassandra." Billy countered his caustic criticism by writing him a letter, praising his ingenuity and offering as he always did to meet him for a "chat." Conner mocked him by inviting Billy to a pub where profane drinkers gathered. He dared Billy to show up.

A few days later "Cassandra" wrote in his column:

> [Billy Graham has] a kind of ferocious cordiality that scares ordinary sinners stone cold. . . . He came into the Baptist's Head [pub] absolutely at home—a teetotaler and an abstainer able to make himself completely at home in the spit and sawdust. . .a difficult thing to do. I never thought that friendliness had such a sharp-cutting edge. I never thought that simplicity could cudgel us sinners so damned hard. We live and learn. . . . The bloke means every thing he says.[3]

The Archbishop of Canterbury, who had shunned the crusade, also repented with stunning praise for Billy:

> [The success of the crusade] is due in the first place to the great humility and sincerity of Dr. Graham himself. . . . He would take or assume nothing for himself, but was clearly a humble man seeking only to use to the utmost of his ability such vision of truth and such gift of expressing it as God had given him.[4]

Billy had in some measure gained the confidence of the archbishop and Britain's Council of Churches. That was important if he was to return. But two other endorsements would have put him at the top of the mountain: the queen and the prime minister. Both seemed highly unlikely. The young Queen Elizabeth II had barely ascended the throne. She was under a microscope and would surely get no advice to embrace an American evangelist. On the other hand, Winston Churchill was immersed in the business of running the British Empire. Surely he was oblivious to any visiting evangelist.

On the last day of the crusade, Billy spoke to crowds of 67,000 and 120,000 in stadiums at White City and Wembley. Between sermons, Billy was as limp as a rag with fatigue but rallied to preach strongly at Wembley. The day was such a stupendous success, the Archbishop of Canterbury seemed dazed in Wembley Stadium as he murmured, "I don't think we'll ever see a sight like this again until we get to heaven."

He was quickly brought crashing down to earth when Grady Wilson threw his arm around him and hooted, "That's right, Brother Archbishop! That's right!"[5]

The colossal success at Wembley triggered a prize invitation. Churchill wanted to meet Billy. Apparently he wanted to see how this American evangelist was enchanting the British people. At noon on May 24, 1954, Billy found himself inside Number 10 Downing Street walking into the Cabinet room.

Churchill stood waiting by a long conference table, toying with an unlit cigar. He had given Billy only five minutes, but he seemed nervous at that. *What in the world does one say to a wild and woolly evangelist?* he seemed to be thinking. In a room lit only by grim overcast daylight seeping in the windows, Churchill had Billy sit across the long table from him. He made a few halfhearted comments about how Britain needed an emphasis on religion.

"Is there any hope for this world?" Churchill asked suddenly.

Billy was shocked. Was this the giant whose immemorial speeches gave the British people hope against the Nazi war machine that seemed unstoppable? Had Churchill at last succumbed to pessimism himself? Or was he testing Billy?

Billy reached in his coat pocket and pulled out his New Testament. "Mr. Prime Minister, this fills me with hope!"

Churchill countered by gesturing at a stack of well-read newspapers on the table. "When I was a boy, a murder was a tragedy everyone talked about for fifty years. Now people are murdered every day. I am an old man, with no hope for the world. Communism is consuming the earth like a wildfire. Are we soon to be hurling hydrogen bombs at each other?"

"I am filled with hope," answered Billy. He waved the New Testament. "This tells me what is going to happen in the future." And Billy punched out the message of Christ in his simple, direct logic. God made man in Christ—Christ the God-man died for our sins. All any man has to do is come to the cross and be born again. Miraculously, Churchill allowed Billy to talk on and on.

Occasionally, Churchill would mutter again, "I am an old man, and I have no hope for the world."

Their mutual sincerity became crystal clear. Churchill was truly pessimistic about the future of mankind. Billy was truly optimistic about the future with Christ. After forty minutes of Billy preaching, with Churchill occasionally interjecting pessimism, the prime minister made it clear the interview was over.

But as they parted, Churchill said, "I do not see much hope for the world unless it is the hope you are talking about. We must return to God." Then he added, "You will keep this conversation private, I trust?"

Billy left, telling reporters only that he felt like he had talked to "Mr. History." And later as he reflected, he realized Churchill was just months short of being eighty years old, probably exhausted from trying to run an empire. Someone had said, "Fatigue makes cowards of us all." Yes, Churchill was a very old, very tired man.

In London, Billy had preached to two million people, either in person or by relay! Nearly forty thousand had come to the altar. The success was staggering in its magnitude. Once again, as he had experienced in Boston four years earlier, he felt a compulsion to remain. Why couldn't he stay and follow through? The revival was well under way. Who knows what might happen if people were reminded of the cross day after day after day? Wasn't that constant practice of God's presence a necessary step to Christian perfection?

On the other hand, as always, he was scheduled to go other places. Could he let those places down? And something else bothered him: Were people attracted to Billy Graham instead of Christ? That bothered him a great deal, as it had ever since Los Angeles. If he stayed in London, didn't he risk enhancing his own image, instead of leading people to the cross? What if a "Billy Graham sect" formed? After discussing the matter with the Archbishop of Canterbury, he decided it was better to come back to England another time.

"Let the English clerics shepherd the new flock," Billy told himself.

He pushed on to Scandinavia. He preached successful one-day meetings in Helsinki, Stockholm, and Copenhagen. Stockholm had a turnout of 65,000. He went on to Amsterdam to preach to 40,000. At each stop, the Navigators followed up on the roughly 2 percent who came to the altar to inquire. Then the European trip began to unravel in Germany. Local ministers had resisted the Navigators, automatically assuming the response to Billy's appeal would be zero.

In Dusseldorf, Billy awoke in the night with wracking pain. A doctor diagnosed a kidney stone. Billy must rest. But he couldn't pass up his next stop: Berlin. It was too important. The symbolism was gigantic. The crusade organizers had reserved mammoth Olympic Stadium, the very stadium where Hitler had postured in 1936. And most important, the East German Communists were frantic. The Communists had launched a virulent propaganda campaign against him, accusing him of being a spy, a hypocrite who swilled alcohol and chased women. Billy couldn't back down.

"I must go ahead to Berlin," he told the team.

The pain returned with a vengeance. The only relief was a pain-killer, which Billy refused to take because he feared it would make him groggy. He couldn't preach in Olympic Stadium in a drugged stupor. And he realized once again God was sending him a message. Billy was puffed up by his astounding success in London. Now when Billy was weak and in pain, he would be spiritually strong anyway. Because he spoke through the Holy Spirit. That afternoon he preached to eighty thousand at Olympic Stadium. Officials were able to estimate how many of those were East Germans because of the number of buses from East Berlin. There were twenty thousand East

Berliners! No wonder the East German Communists had smeared him. Their captives were starved for God. Billy's short, punchy sentences were ideal for a translated sermon. Thousands of Germans started to surge forward when Billy invited them to the altar. He had to act immediately. He told them the crusade team would not be able to counsel so many at once. He urged them to write letters so local pastors would follow up.

As he left Berlin, a supporter told him, "The Communists are already spreading more lies about you. You're a hypocrite who caroused in East Berlin night clubs with the money you collected. And you left without paying your hotel bill."

Billy sighed. "Let me tell you, friend. The devil starts many deliberate lies about God's servants. And a lot of poor folks will believe the lies and pass them on as gossip. I make it a point never to answer gossip if I can help it. The devil would like nothing better than to have me stop bringing men to Christ and try to track down every lie and try to dispute it."[6]

A few days later in Paris, in spite of searing pain, he preached well again. His sermon was so well received, the team began planning a crusade for Paris. After that, he returned to North Carolina, where he had an operation for the kidney stone. Mercifully, the doctor ordered him to rest at home for six weeks. He was run down and underweight. The results of the Berlin crusade sped his recovery. Over sixteen thousand letters had been sent in by inquirers! What better evidence could be found of the spiritual hunger in Germany?

In March 1955, Billy once again crossed the Atlantic, this time for his All-Scotland Crusade. This crusade was officially supported by the churches. The support was not lukewarm, either, but steamy hot. Scotland was in the grips of a wave of evangelism among its clergy. All reserved seats in Kelvin Hall, the site of the crusade in Glasgow, were booked solid for all six weeks. Because of such support, expectations were very high. And it had already yielded one innovation for future crusades.

The training of counselors reached a new high. First, the clergy from all over Scotland came to Glasgow to take classes. About six hundred came. Armed with certain knowledge of what was taught to the counselors, the clergy recruited members of their congregations to attend. In all, over four thousand volunteer counselors were trained for the crusade.

"The training is so effective," his hosts told Billy, "that some of the volunteers came to realize they needed to be born again themselves."

Because the organizers fully expected Kelvin Hall to be full every meeting, they arranged to seat the overflow in a nearby auditorium that received a televised version of the meeting. As with many crusades, Billy had a dark moment at the beginning. This All-Scotland Crusade, wholeheartedly supported by the churches, had such lofty expectations. And if he reflected too much, he was always overwhelmed by his own role. Why had he been so blessed? Why had God picked him?

But another element bothered him before the first meeting. His hosts warned him, "We Scots do not come to the altar. Inquirers normally wait in the back of the church or are discretely shunted into a side room."

Should Billy try his usual method? Would Scots come to Christ so publicly? Several clergy advised him not to try it. Why risk it? But Billy, in spite of periods of nail-biting doubt, was always a risk-taker. He took a deep breath and called them forward at the first meeting. There was such a flood of Scots rushing to the altar, clergy on the platform with Billy were crying.

The crusade never wavered. The response night after night was so gratifying that the organizers expanded their crusade by telephoned broadcasts into England, Ireland, and Wales. During Easter week, the meetings were also televised and radioed to other parts of Scotland by a network far more sophisticated than the one hastily rigged at Harringay Arena the previous year.

"Are you ready for the finale?" asked Grady, trying to act nonchalant.

"If the Holy Spirit is," answered Billy nervously.

The climax was the Good Friday meeting where Billy was accessible by BBC television to virtually all of Britain! He had fretted about it for a week. They were saying only Queen Elizabeth's coronation had been watched by so many British. It was going to be watched from pubs to Buckingham Palace. All morning of Good Friday, he read and reread the Bible's four stories of the crucifixion. Christ's suffering floored him. That night Billy was sure he spoke through the Holy Spirit on the meaning of the cross.

People were talking about it the next day. Reviews were glowing. Later he was honored by the General Assembly of the Church of Scotland. The crusade was over, a success admitted by the most begrudging observer in every aspect but one: lasting results. Each of Billy's crusades was now picked apart in retrospect. How many inquirers actually went on to become church members? How many were still church members five years later? Objective skeptics—and supporters—had to admit the results defied analysis. The impact could not be measured. Who could say how many nominal Christians were changed into true Christians by the crusade? Or vice versa?

"I prefer to think of myself as a revivalist," admitted Billy with his usual complete honesty. "Who can say how many have actually been converted through my preaching?"

Billy went on to England, where he held a seven-night crusade in Wembley Stadium. He was apprehensive. Was it too soon to return to England? His critics were silent. That bothered him, too. His London critics seemed almost devilishly quiet. He did not fill the stadium every night. And that was what the critics jumped on: The glass was half empty. A turnout of eighty thousand became through their eyes a failure to fill all the seats. And once again, he was not endorsed by the Church of England. No official attended any of the meetings.

"Stop moping, Billy. Don't forget our invitation," reminded Ruth.

"Praise God for that," agreed Billy. "I must not diminish that blessing even if we do have to keep it a secret."

ELEVEN

Billy and Ruth had been invited to meet with the Queen Mother and Princess Margaret. From them, Billy learned the royal family had been following his activity very closely. They even knew details about his family life. Five days later, in strictest confidence, he was allowed to preach to young Queen Elizabeth and her retinue at Windsor Castle.

He preached on chapter 27 of Acts, building his sermon around Paul's statement of faith after the angel visited him on the sinking Alexandrian ship: "So keep up your courage, men, for I have faith in God that it will happen just as he told me."

The Grahams stayed for lunch and learned upon returning to London that the queen had made the meeting public. Billy was besieged by reporters. He would tell them nothing. So some made up stories. One fabrication related how Billy patronized Prince Charles by patting him on the head.

"I might have done that if he had been there," admitted

Billy to Ruth. But seven-year-old Prince Charles had not been there.

Billy moved on to Paris for five meetings, then blazed through twelve cities in Switzerland, Germany, Scandinavia, and Holland. He returned to America, then Canada, to hold a crusade in Toronto for three weeks. But Billy was absorbed by presidential politics. President Eisenhower had suffered a stroke. He couldn't even speak. Billy prayed for his full recovery. But he also pondered on his successor. Would it be Adlai Stevenson, his challenger in 1952? Or would it be Ike's vice president, Richard Nixon? Whereas Stevenson seemed transparently an affable but very liberal Democrat, Nixon was opaque. Some hated him. Some adored him. Billy had been very favorably impressed.

"He's a Quaker," he explained to Ruth. "They are very quiet about their religious views."

Lurking in the back of Billy's mind was a November meeting at Cambridge University in England. He was scheduled to preach to very high-powered theologians. Billy had little formal theological training. He remembered only too well how Chuck Templeton, with his small amount of theological training, had tied him in knots in discussions.

The more Billy thought about Cambridge, the more panicky he became. He couldn't cancel. That just wasn't his way. It would show in no uncertain terms lack of trust in God. His apprehension was widely known after a while. The Bishop of Barking wrote him from England, advising him to speak to the people at Cambridge as sinners, not intellectuals.

But Billy remained so nervous about the Cambridge trip that when he saw his old friend Stephen Olford, he recruited him on his knees to tutor him. Olford agreed. And Billy crammed theological maxims day after day, so he could be as nimble-minded as the gifted John Stott, who would assist Billy in the meetings.

"You should be speaking," he told Stott when he arrived at Cambridge.

After the first three meetings, Billy knew no one at Cambridge was aware how much he had altered his message. Oh, they knew he was nervous. But they thought it was their restrictive format. They thought he was missing his team of Grady Wilson, Cliff Barrows, and Bev Shea. They were actually pleasantly surprised at his theological acumen. They expected no theological sparks. But Billy knew he was not reaching their hearts.

On the next occasion, a faculty member chilled Billy by introducing him with the remark he could not agree with his doctrinal views. Billy shrugged off theological hair-splitting. "If a minister can't win souls for Christ, he is not a minister, no matter how well versed he is in theology."[1] The startled students began cheering.

And the fireworks began. Finally Billy took the advice he had received from the Bishop of Barking. The real Billy, the unrelenting evangelist, began pointing his finger at the sinners and making them squirm. The tears of remorse came, followed by the trips to the altar. But the meetings were soon over. Why hadn't he done that sooner? He resolved never again to let a college audience intimidate him into abandoning his message.

In early 1956, Billy traveled to India. The trip had been engineered by the English. Once again, measured by the size of the crowds he attracted, Billy was successful. But in his own mind, the trip was successful only because he recruited a man named Akbar Abdul-Haqq. Billy would bring him to America and train him to lead his own crusades in India. Turnouts of one hundred thousand, with little advance preparation, proved the Indians were receptive.

"I've never seen such spontaneous hunger for God," commented Billy.

Before Billy left India, he met the prime minister, Jawaharlal Nehru. Billy was apprehensive because he knew Nehru's India was doing what many countries were doing at that time. They were cozying up to Russia in order to extract massive foreign aid from the United States. Nehru's coldness made it plain from the outset this meeting with Billy had no merit in his eyes. Billy showered Nehru with compliments about how Americans loved India. Nehru refused to respond. Finally Billy told Nehru about Christ. The prime minister showed mild interest. Billy assured him any missionary activity for Christ would stay completely away from politics. Nehru almost became cordial.

Billy made one-day stops in the Philippines, Korea, Hong Kong, Formosa, Japan, and Hawaii. When he returned to America, President Eisenhower, who had made a wonderful recovery, said at a press conference that Billy Graham was a man who understood "any advance in the world has got to be accompanied by a clear realization that man is, after all, a spiritual being."[2]

At Montreat, Billy got a surprise. Ruth and the children were in a new home. Ruth called it "Little Piney Cove." It was located on the property Billy and Ruth had bought on the mountain several years earlier. Ruth drove Billy to it on a winding road in a jeep.

"Are you sure you want to be way up here on the mountain?" asked Billy.

"Ever since the Harringay trip, the tourists haven't left us alone."

Billy knew it was true. It wasn't just an occasional car that slowed on Assembly Drive so everyone inside the car could gawk. No, since 1954, chartered buses stopped to unload tourists. Some of them would ask to take pictures of the Graham children. Ruth was very upset. And when she caught Bunny opening her small red purse to solicit money for pictures, she decided then and there they had to move.

Now the Grahams lived at Little Piney Cove, with a view of Black Mountain and the Swannanoa Valley. The new house was U-shaped, of log construction, totally Ruth's creation. She had scrounged used lumber from old cabins so it would be authentically rustic. All walls were exposed timber. Her biggest problem was getting artisans to do as she wanted. In their minds, her requests were crazy. The new ceiling she wanted had to show trowel marks in the plaster. The rock wall could not show any mortar. More than one craftsman stomped off the job. But Ruth persisted.

The kitchen was very large with a hearth and a brick floor. The living room and dining room each had a fireplace and faced the pine-studded valley below. From the brick-floored porch on the front of the house down to a split-rail fence stretched a lawn. The bedrooms looked up the mountainside, where thorny blackberry bushes fringed pine, aspen, and maple trees. Billy and Ruth both had studies on the first floor, but Ruth's was a small study in one corner of the master bedroom. Her main object of study was her Bible, which she treated with great tenderness. But she had to replace its tattered pages every ten years anyway. The second floor was the domain of the children. Ruth kept her visits to a minimum to make sure they were cleaning their rooms.

After one incident, Billy never went upstairs unless invited. He had followed GiGi, who had stormed up to her room and slammed the door after an argument. He entered her room and scolded her for her rudeness. She snapped, "Some dad you are! You're never here."

Billy felt like she had slapped his face. His heart ached. What could he say? She was right. He was rarely there. After that, he felt like a hypocrite trying to discipline the kids the strict way his father had disciplined him. His father was not a hypocrite; he was always there.

GiGi was almost eleven; Anne, eight; Bunny, five; and Franklin, three. Billy knew their family life was unusual. When he came home, Ruth deferred to his idea of discipline. But after the incident with GiGi, Billy was far more lax than Ruth, except about Sunday. Then the children could have no visitors, no television, no games. It was a day only for worship, prayer, and meditation—just as it had been so many years ago on the farm. The children hinted crudely that if Billy would stay home during the week and travel on weekends, life would be perfect.

Rain on the mountain was frequent. Soft rain seemed wonderful to Ruth; it depressed Billy. When he fretted and gnawed his fingernails, as he always did, the children dubbed him "Puddleglum," a lovable but constantly pessimistic character in *The Silver Chair* by C. S. Lewis. "Is the King dead? Has the enemy landed in Narnia?" giggled the children. They had read all the "Narnia" books by Lewis. So did Ruth. And she branched out into the realm of Lewis, reading his adult books and his taste in other writers: George MacDonald and G. K. Chesterton. She even collected discarded first editions signed by them.

"Someday maybe these saintly authors will be appreciated," she told Billy.

It was a long, hot summer. The issue of racial injustice was simmering. Blacks no longer would submit to separate seating, separate water fountains, separate schools, and high poll taxes to discourage them from voting. Billy had discussed the problems with Ike. Both agreed the injustices were intolerable. But both agreed white southerners had to be nudged along. Strong-arm policies were dangerous.

"The hearts of bigots have to be changed first," warned Billy.

Billy went about it. He phoned the governors of North Carolina and Tennessee to urge them to address the racial problems from a spiritual point of view and promote justice. Then he phoned or met with prominent white and black religious leaders in the South.

His viewpoint became well known. "If the extremists on both sides will just cool down, we can have a nice peaceful adjustment of black equality over the next ten years." Response to his moderation was swift. He was attacked from integrationists on one side and segregationists on the other.

His great friend Dawson Trotman drowned in a boating accident in New York. Trotman would be missed for practical reasons, too. No one knew how to nurture babes in Christ as well as Trotman and his Navigators. And it reminded Billy of his own mortality. What did he have left to do?

Since Christmas 1954, Billy and his father-in-law, Nelson Bell, had talked about a magazine for evangelicals similar to *Christian Century*, the magazine liberal Christians had published for many years. Billy could never forget *Christian Century* for very long because the secular press quoted it constantly as if it were the only respectable religious publication. And it lambasted Billy constantly. Billy had no thoughts of revenge. It was simply a case of fulfilling a need for evangelicals.

In fall 1955, Nelson Bell resigned his surgical practice to ramrod the magazine, already called *Christianity Today*. By the middle of 1956, Carl Henry was appointed managing editor, although Billy was worried he was too much of an egghead. The first issue was scheduled for fall 1956. Billy was tempted to make the magazine the official voice of BGEA. Finally he decided that would diminish the magazine's broad appeal. Still, he served on its board. And he sent a scathing critique of the first issue to Carl Henry. He wrote it was "not strikingly good, considering the terrific roster of editors and correspondents. . . . I felt like you would like to know the hard, cold facts."[3]

In many ways Billy felt *Christianity Today* was the last cog in the evangelical machine he had built, even if the magazine was semi-independent. He spread the gospel in crusades, movies, radio, television, a newspaper column, and a book. Surely that was diverse enough. He didn't have to completely control the magazine, too. Nelson Bell and Carl Henry were as true "new evangelicals" as he was.

People were even calling Billy's movement the New Evangelicalism. It was an effort to distinguish it from Fundamentalism. In his heart, Billy believed Fundamentalism. Just like Fundamentalists, Billy believed that Scripture was true and inspired by God; that man's original sin was true; that Christ was born of a virgin; that Christ's divinity, atonement, resurrection, and Second Coming were all true.

· The problem lay with a handful of intolerant Fundamentalists who gave Fundamentalism a bad name. Billy believed men had to be tolerant of other beliefs. Evangelicals had to love liberal Christians and try to persuade them, not fight them. He knew there was some biblical foundation for the combative style of a few Fundamentalists like Carl McIntire. After all, Jesus had blistered the Pharisees. But Jesus usually tried to persuade His opponents. And Billy had to admit he was skeptical about some of the Fundamentalists' pugilistic attitudes that did not center on Christ's love.

"If folks want to label me a New Evangelical, that's fine with me," said Billy, who never claimed to be the founder of New Evangelicalism but knew he was the most visible.

In November 1956, Ike was reelected easily over Adlai Stevenson. Billy could relax. He still had a good friend in the White House. He became totally absorbed in getting ready for his New York campaign in May 1957. BGEA approached the crusade with complete optimism. They contracted Madison Square Garden for several weeks. But the specter of Billy Sunday was really haunting Billy now. He felt at long last like he was going head-to-head with the legend.

If anyone doubted Billy Sunday was a giant among evangelists, they needed only to review his 1917 crusade in New

York. In a city supposedly too tough to care, he drew 1.5 million people in ten weeks. He claimed a colossal 100,000 inquirers! Billy Graham could hardly comprehend Billy Sunday's claim that in his lifetime he had preached face-to-face to 100 million sinners! And yet when it was explained to him many years ago at the Florida Bible Institute, he had to admit the total was not unreasonable. For forty years, Sunday held six campaigns a year. In each campaign, he delivered fifty sermons, with an average turnout of 10,000.

"If I'm multiplying all those numbers right, the total is over 100 million," said an awed Billy Graham.

The Protestant Council of New York had presented a united front in inviting Billy in 1957. They represented thirty-one denominations and seventeen hundred churches. But New York was the nerve center of the rest of America, too. Billy was immediately attacked from Fundamentalists on the right and the liberal theologian Reinhold Neibuhr on the left. Their attacks seemed nitpicky, but they were unrelenting.

It was soon obvious the results in New York were going to be staggering. Night after night, Billy preached to nearly twenty thousand people. After it was clear he was going to pack the Garden every night, BGEA approached the ABC television network to buy airtime for nationwide Saturday night specials. The first one on June 1 competed with television giants Jackie Gleason and Perry Como on the other two networks. Billy got only 20 percent of the total viewers. He was a distant third, yet he reached an astounding six million viewers! The power of television was awesome.

The reviewer in the entertainment newspaper *Variety* wrote:

Few performers, whether on TV, stage or film, have the dynamic qualities of Graham or are as sure of them-selves. . . . There's no unctuous quality, no sanctimo-nious persuasion. The voice is strong. . . . He's a man of perpetual motion [but] the constant gesturing is never accidental, for the vast sweep of both his hands and arms propels and holds the attention. . . . The voice never falters, never gropes for a word or a phrase and is as assured as his beliefs.

BGEA began to get fifty thousand letters a week. Billy topped himself in New York week after week. He appeared as a guest on all the network news shows. Celebrities were drawn to the revivals like flies to honey: Walter Winchell, Ed Sullivan, Edward G. Robinson, John Wayne, Pearl Bailey, Jack Dempsey, Sonja Henie, Dorothy Kilgallen, Gene Tierney, Greer Garson, Ethel Waters.

Howard Jones, a black evangelical at BGEA, arranged for Billy to speak at a black church in Harlem. And in an inspired move, Billy invited the Reverend Martin Luther King, the black civil rights leader, to open one service at the Garden in prayer. As usual, Billy's approach to the race prob-lems was low-key. He did not harangue the audience after-ward, but let the notion soak in that whites and blacks work together for God. His comments in magazines were more blunt: Hating anyone because of the color of his skin is a sin.

Nearing the end of sixteen weeks in New York, Ruth was worried about Billy. "How much do you weigh now? Your suits bag on you."

"I've lost over thirty pounds," admitted Billy. "But 'I can

do everything through him who gives me strength,' " he added, quoting Philippians 4:13, one of his favorite verses.

But some days he felt like he might not ever recover from New York. Luckily, the revival was drawing to a close. He had preached to over 2 million people, getting 55,000 inquirers for Christ. But he wasn't through yet. He drew 100,000 into Yankee Stadium. And for his finale drew 200,000 people into Times Square. His total of 2.3 million had topped the great Billy Sunday's New York revival! His popularity was so colossal, it frightened him.

"To God be all the glory," Billy assured the team. "This is His doing, and let no one fail to give Him the credit."

When Billy returned to Little Piney Cove, GiGi had left for Hampden-Dubose, a Christian boarding school in Florida. Ruth was adamant. There was too much sin in the local public school. Besides, her parents had packed her off to a Christian school in Korea at the age of twelve. And Ruth at thirty-seven was five months' pregnant.

His return home was not relaxing. The outside world would not leave him alone. Racial problems were ablaze everywhere. Even in Billy's own hometown of Charlotte, a black girl had been harassed for trying to go to all-white Harding High School. Billy quickly wrote her a letter, urging her to "hold fast and carry on. . . . You have been chosen. Those cowardly whites against you will never prosper. . . . Be of good faith. . . . [God] will see you through."[4]

Then a confrontation caught the entire nation's attention. Arkansas governor Faubus was going to defy the Supreme Court's 1954 ruling that schools had to desegregate. He refused to allow blacks to enter Central High School in Little Rock. On the pretext that he was preventing violence, he stationed 270 National Guardsmen at the high school.

Billy told a newspaper reporter, "It is the duty of every Christian, when it does not violate his relationship with God, to obey the law."[5] And Billy made it plain: Faubus was in the wrong. Bigotry was a sin.

One morning Billy got a phone call from the White House. The president had been consulting him for some time on racial matters. Ike respected moral authority based on the Bible. And Billy knew the Bible. But this time Ike sought more. He wanted to know what a moral white southerner thought of the situation in Little Rock. Ike was feeling Billy out about sending troops to Little Rock.

"Do it, Mr. President."

Within an hour, Vice President Nixon called Billy to ask the same question.

"Do it," answered Billy.

That afternoon the 101st Airborne Division entered Little Rock. Central High School was desegregated.

What in the world could Billy do to top 1957?

TWELVE

As 1958 began, Billy toyed with the idea of establish-ing a college. No college emphasized the broad band of evangelicalism that Billy believed. There was no lack of enthusiasm for the idea. At the mere mention of a possible college near New York, supporters flocked to his aid: Vice President Nixon, former New York governor Thomas Dewey, radio commentator Paul Harvey. But it soon became appar-ent this support assumed he would be the keystone of the new school. His experience at Northwestern Bible School taught him he was no college administrator. Nor, in his heart, did he want to be.

"Besides, it seems a little indulgent now," he confided to Ruth. "Racial injustices need to be pushed front and center."

He was already doing for that issue what he did best. Constant verbal and written attacks on him by the Ku Klux Klan and the White Citizens Council proved he was hitting them where it hurt. He would attest loud and clear that bigotry was a sin. He would show support for black leaders like Martin Luther King, as long as they were pacifists. But in his heart, he knew the black leaders were doing it best. And he feared a faster pace might set the South on fire.

His cup seemed full. A second son, Nelson Edman, was born January 12 and immediately dubbed "Ned." Besides crusades, Billy had to maintain outlets in newspapers, books, radio, television, and movies. He mothered *Christianity Today* as a member of its board. He was always adding new people to his BGEA staff. He had recently talked T. W. Wilson, Grady's brother, into joining the crusade team. T. W., after doing the heavy work at Northwestern Bible School for Billy, had left for a while on his own evangelical career.

Closest to his evangelical heart, Billy worked on refining crusades. Few people appreciated how much time was actually devoted to a crusade. Praying, organizing workers, and training counselors started months ahead of the actual meetings. That part of the crusade process satisfied Billy. Actual counseling after the crusade, pioneered by Dawson Trotman, was well known in concept but not as well executed. The real bottleneck in the evangelical process was turning the babes in Christ over to the churches. The inefficiency of that step was heartbreaking. He knew what the churches would say. The conversions were so superficial, there was not enough time for the process to work.

"Somehow we must inspire the churches to go after the babes in Christ with more tender loving care," said Billy.

The team went to Central America for three weeks, San Francisco for seven weeks, Sacramento for one week, and Charlotte for several weeks. Those crusades sprouted more opportunities. In San Francisco, Billy's message converted minister Sherwood Wirt from a devotee of liberal theology to an evangelical. Wirt was a man of many talents. With a doctorate from the University of Edinburgh, he also had once edited a newspaper. With Billy's encouragement, he wrote articles about the San Francisco crusade for *Christianity Today*, then started writing a book on the crusade.

Billy's mind was cranking. "I still want a small magazine as the official voice of BGEA. Sherwood is very able."

That fall, racists bombed a high school in Clinton, Tennessee. The school had just been desegregated. Billy stepped forward to declare, "Every Christian should take his stand against these outrages." In December he spoke in Clinton to an audience of five thousand to raise money for a new school, calling, as he always did in his own heart, for "forgiveness, cool heads, and warm hearts."

One day in January 1959 when Billy was playing golf, his club head kept missing the ball. "The ground has ridges in it," he explained to Grady.

Grady chuckled. "Lord have mercy. That's a new excuse, buddy."

Suddenly, pain stabbed Billy's left eye.

At the Mayo Clinic, they found that Billy suffered edema in his left eye. Preparation for a new crusade was well under way. The team was going to Australia and New Zealand in just a few weeks. Billy was ordered to rest. His schedule in Australia was pared back. He rested in Hawaii with Ruth and the Grady Wilsons. But he was not idle. Raymond Edman came to him from Wheaton College. All of them took a crash course on the Bible.

"This is surely God's way of making me recharge my spiritual batteries," said Billy. "Maybe I've taken Australia too lightly."

In those days in Hawaii, he established a routine for Bible reading that he hoped would stay with him forever. Every day he read five Psalms and enough of Proverbs so that he would read each book completely every month. Proverbs instructed him how to deal with his fellow men. Psalms inspired him to talk to God. In addition, he read enough of the rest of Scripture each day to get completely through the Bible once each year.

When he opened in Melbourne in February 1959, pessimists said there just wasn't enough population in Australia to mount huge crowds. But pessimists didn't appreciate how well the team had prepared Australia and how enthusiastically the churches promoted the crusade. The crusade had to move immediately from a 10,000-seat facility to a sprawling outdoor amphitheater where crowds swelled to 25,000 and finally to 70,000. At Melbourne's finale at the Cricket Ground, turnstiles reached 130,000 before police simply opened other gates to relieve the incoming flood of people.

In Sydney, Billy preached to 70,000 in their Cricket Ground with speakers reaching another 80,000 in an adjacent Showground. Sidney added a new innovation for the crusades. They dubbed it pre-crusade, citywide visitation. In plain English, they knocked on every door of every house in Sydney, inviting the residents to the crusade!

In just four weeks, Billy preached to one million Australians. He felt he was watching the power of the Holy Spirit. The turnouts were not his doing, not even within his control.

God was at work. He was sure of it. He stopped in England on his way back to America. The queen wanted a firsthand report of his success in the far reaches of the British Empire.

"I was amazed at the great spiritual depth of Australia and New Zealand," Billy told Queen Elizabeth and Prince Philip over tea. "All is well Down Under."

Back in America, Billy held two rallies in Little Rock. Racist groups mounted hate campaigns against him. But Governor Faubus was shrewd. He urged segregationists to leave him alone. Billy was just too popular. And Billy, practicing the gospel of love, talked to everyone, trying to heal Little Rock of its bitterness. At the crusade meetings, local pastors were stunned to see avowed racists coming to the altar. Little Rock was desegregated—and recovering.

At home, timid Anne was now the oldest child at eleven. Mild-mannered Bunny had just turned nine, a few weeks before Ned would turn two. Franklin was seven and seemed destined to replace GiGi as the instigator of mischief. How he loved to badger Ned. At times Ruth was so desperate, she studied a book on training dogs. Her solutions as a parent were definitely not orthodox. Once on the way to a drive-in restaurant, she locked quarrelsome Franklin in the trunk of the car. In Asheville, he emerged from the trunk unrepentant, with the poise of a cat burglar. "I'll have a cheeseburger. Hold the onions."

The next year, 1960, was a year of great temptation for Billy. Oh, how he wanted to meddle in the 1960 election! Ike could not run again for president. The Republicans would surely nominate Billy's friend Richard Nixon. Since 1956, Billy had indulged in political strategies with Nixon, confiding what he thought would happen if Nixon were to run against this

Democrat or that Democrat. If it was John Kennedy, what should Nixon do? Or if it was Lyndon Johnson, what should Nixon do? And what if some dark horse got the nomination?

"Running for president is as exciting as a horse race, for sure!" Billy cried.

"Stay out of politics," said wet-blanket Ruth.

But Billy knew dabbling in politics was wrong for his ministry, too. His friendship with Ike's White House had gotten out of hand. That was why he had earlier decided that 1960 was going to be a year abroad. He started in Africa in January. The crusade through Africa skipped the most powerful country on the continent: South Africa. When Billy found out that blacks could not attend his rallies and that his own black evangelist Howard Jones would have problems rooming and eating there, the crusade abandoned South Africa. When those conditions could be met, he would go there.

He began in Liberia, where Howard Jones evangelized several months every year. Billy began with John 3:16, the very essence of the gospel: "For God so loved the world that he gave his one and only Son, that whoever believes in him shall not perish but have eternal life."

Then he told them how that son, Jesus, had been born near Africa. He had found refuge as a child in Africa. He was not European-looking at all but dark-skinned and dark-eyed. The Libyan Simon had helped Jesus carry His cross. Billy felt those connections helped the Africans open their hearts to Christ. But for the team, the turnouts in Liberia were low, a few thousand every day.

The turnouts were low in Ghana, too. Billy had lambasted both Communists and Muslims in the past, so it was no surprise they campaigned against him in Ghana. In Nigeria, Billy drew large crowds, over one hundred thousand in one week. At Kaduna in Nigeria, he was invited to a leper colony. He found the lepers had built him an arbor of limbs and brush. He steeled himself against the sight of faces eaten away. He preached to them, assuring them that God loved them. A new spiritual body awaited them in heaven. Billy hadn't ached for such suffering since Korea. As he was about to leave, a small maimed woman shuffled toward him, extending an envelope with fingerless hands. A missionary told Billy the lepers had taken up a love offering for his ministry.

"Boys," he told Grady and Cliff brightly, "that's what the ministry is all about."[1] But Billy couldn't keep the hot tears back. It was one of the most bittersweet moments of his life. God had let him meet the widow in Luke 21. Billy was so undeserving.

The Muslims had managed to have his invitation to Sudan withdrawn, so he went on to Kenya, Tanganyika, and Rhodesia. Turnouts were mainly white. These countries were in the grip of rebellion. Black Africans were trying to throw out white colonists. And even though the white-controlled governments showcased certain blacks who made good money, Billy could see the blacks were very unhappy.

He said of South Africa's apartheid, "To keep the races in total separation is immoral and un-Christian."

He was received with open arms in Ethiopia, a country with a Christian tradition back to the apostle Phillip. In Egypt, Billy learned a full-scale crusade might be possible. But he decided it would be too provocative in an overwhelmingly Muslim country. Muslims were much more hostile than Hindus. He visited Jordan, whose king made it clear he was being pressured into seeing him. He was not welcome.

In Israel, he was not allowed to hold public meetings. And he was warned not to so much as mention the name of Jesus to any Jew. But Billy made the most of his time. He felt he convinced influential Israeli politicians Abba Eban and Golda Meir that he was a true friend of Israel. He was always patient. There would be another opportunity.

To reporters and in private correspondence, he was not judgmental about Africa. After past crusades, unguarded comments had erased a lot of the goodwill he and the team had worked so hard to generate. That had happened in India. Billy let a reporter quote from letters he wrote home to Ruth. Some of his blunt judgments enraged the Indians.

In Washington, D.C., Billy briefed Ike, Vice President Nixon, and the Secretary of State on his trip. He confided, "I'm worried that the suppression of blacks in Africa is causing them to turn to Communism."

Now that he was back in America, Billy was nagged by the temptation to support Nixon openly. Nixon's chances of winning the presidential election seemed less every day. The popularity of John Kennedy was running so high, it appeared he would win the Democratic nomination on the first ballot. Ike's own reservations about Nixon were not comforting to Billy. What did Ike see about Nixon that Billy could not see? Oh, Richard Nixon was not photogenic and he seemed rarely at ease. But his goals were sound. And Kennedy was such a rake with women. He dishonored his own house. As far as Billy knew, America had never had such a man as president.

Billy couldn't keep from making pointed comments in public like, "I don't think it's time to experiment with novices."[2]

Finally Billy offered to come out openly for Nixon on *Meet the Press* in June. Nixon demurred. "Stay out of politics," he advised. But in black moments, Billy wondered if Nixon had weighed all the pros and cons of Billy's support and decided Billy would cost him votes. In a letter to Nixon in June, Billy offered his advice on running mates. "Don't bother to pick a Catholic to vie with Kennedy for Catholic votes," urged Billy. "Kennedy has a lock on 90 percent of them anyway. Pick a Protestant who appeals to the broad spectrum of Protestants." Billy recommended Walter Judd, a congressman from Asheville. He added he would consider it a favor if Nixon destroyed the letter.

"Why am I wondering if Nixon will do it?" he asked himself.

Kennedy discretely asked many well-known clergymen to pledge to remain silent on religion during the campaign. Grady Wilson popped off about the pledge on a radio program. Kennedy's press secretary immediately denied Kennedy had asked any such thing.

"Politics," muttered Billy, now glad that after the team held a one-week crusade in Washington, D.C., and he attended a conference in Brazil, the national conventions would be over.

By the time he returned to America, the nominees were picked. Nixon was running with New Englander Henry Cabot Lodge. Lodge was supposed to compete with Kennedy for votes in the East. Kennedy had picked Lyndon Johnson of Texas to make sure the southern states, which always voted Democratic, did not defect because Kennedy was a Catholic.

Billy had not escaped politics in Brazil. He had talked with Martin Luther King during the trip, and he was very alarmed. In 1956, Ike got 60 percent of the black vote. Billy learned from King the blacks liked Kennedy very much. He also learned King had met with Kennedy. Billy urged Nixon to talk to King. Nixon demurred.

Billy was drawn right back into the campaign. He just couldn't seem to resist. He found himself urging Ike to campaign for Nixon across the South, not the Deep South but states like Kentucky and Texas that Ike had won in 1956. He also suggested Ike openly combat the Democratic congress to steal the thunder from the campaign.

"I can't seem to stay out of it," said Billy to Ruth.

But Billy was not alone in what almost seemed a compulsion to meddle in the 1960 election. Norman Vincent Peale came out for Nixon. A Methodist who was the president of the World Council of Churches voiced concern over how independent a Catholic president could be from the Vatican. And a Presbyterian who was president of the National Council of Churches expressed similar concerns.

Billy began to wonder just how much of his own support for Nixon was really bigotry against a Catholic. Surely, he told himself, he simply wanted to see Nixon elected. He began to back off. He was very grateful now he would be crusading in Europe all of August and September. The election drew him like a moth to a flame. He couldn't keep out of it. And other religious leaders were drawn to it, too.

"We're not leaving for Europe any too soon," said Ruth.

She was very excited about Billy's next trip. In Switzerland, where Billy would crusade for one month, the entire Graham family were guests of Ara Tchividjian, a wealthy man converted through Billy's book *Peace with God*. Billy preached one-week revivals in Berne, Basal, and Lausanne. Then he preached two days in Zurich.

After Switzerland, Billy returned to Germany. The finale of a one-week crusade was right by the Brandenburg Gate in front of the old Reichstag building where the Nazis flaunted their oversized swastika. In a huge tent, Billy preached to twenty-five thousand Germans, many from East Germany. He held up the Bible and said, pausing after every sentence, so it could be translated:

> *Martin Luther was reading this Book when God spoke to him, and it changed the course of history. You come back to this book, begin to read it, study it, and God will speak to you and, through you, perhaps history can be changed [again].*[3]

He resisted speaking out against Communism and inflaming the crowd. He had learned to speak nothing but the truth, while resisting fruitless provocations. Still, the almost laughably incompetent East German press claimed Billy was out enjoying the nightlife of the town with a blond named Bev Shea!

When Billy returned to America, he found that Kennedy had faced the religion question squarely and had even turned it into an advantage. The press now portrayed him as a martyr who was being persecuted. But Billy busied himself with a three-day crusade in New York for Hispanics and getting out the first issue of *Decision*, his new magazine that was blatantly the official magazine for BGEA. *Decision* was edited by Sherwood Wirt, Billy's recruit from the San Francisco crusade. It was much breezier and more partisan than *Christianity Today*.

Holding the new magazine, Billy told Ruth, *"Decision* notes there is a presidential election on the horizon. It goes on to warn its readers that the future course of America could be dangerously altered and the free preaching of the gospel could be endangered. What do you think?"

Ruth's jaw dropped. "I think everyone is going to know those words came right out of your mouth."

"But I'm worried."

Billy became so worried about the election, he offered to write an article for *Life* magazine, not denigrating Kennedy but building up Nixon. Ruth was appalled that he was going so public. Within days, Billy regretted it himself and tried to get Henry Luce to pull the article. But Luce only pulled it after Kennedy got wind of the article and personally complained.

Election night in November was tense. Nixon was winning the West and most of the Midwest. Kennedy was winning the Deep South and a few Midwest states. But Kennedy's Midwest states were big ones: Illinois and Michigan. Billy noted with chagrin his own North Carolina was going for Kennedy. It looked as if Johnson would deliver Texas for Kennedy. Nixon would sweep the West. Two states would make the difference: New York and Pennsylvania. The two held a total 87 electoral votes out of the 269 needed for a majority. Without the two states, Nixon was leading Kennedy 219 to 216.

Complete returns were slow in coming. No one would know for sure who won until the next morning.

THIRTEEN

K ennedy won both states!" cried Billy the next morning. Ike had won New York and Pennsylvania handily, both in 1952 and 1956. But Billy had no time for lamentations. Within two weeks, he was invited to play golf with Kennedy in Florida. But the meeting was delayed because Kennedy's son, John Jr., was born. It was January before Billy finally met with President-elect Kennedy for their game of golf. That evening Kennedy held a press conference, where he unexpectedly called on Billy to address the religious questions still surfacing. So Billy said truthfully that Kennedy's election had breached the gulf between Protestants and Catholics. Religion may never be an issue in a presidential campaign again.

But he felt used. Kennedy was shrewd. If Billy liked politics, the entire Kennedy family reveled in politics. And everyone around Kennedy ate, drank, and slept politics. Every movement was choreographed. This was not going to be a president who was candid.

Billy spent the first four months in Florida, including a three-week crusade in Miami and shorter revivals in other cities. In the spring, Fort Lauderdale's mayor appealed to Billy to calm vacationing college students. Billy had always been effective with students. In England and at Yale, he had defused students hell-bent on mocking his message. He accepted.

"What do you believe in?" he asked the crowd of several thousand partying students on the beach.

"Sex!" screamed the crowd.

"Yes, that's important. Without it, we wouldn't be here today."[1] It was that kind of good-natured reaction to taunting that won people of any age. The students listened to Billy talk about Jesus for an hour.

That April it became painfully apparent the new president was a risk-taker. He approved an invasion of Cuba by Cuban refugees but got cold feet at the last moment and withdrew air support. The invasion was a fiasco. The Communist dictator Castro was stronger than ever, perhaps safe indefinitely. The press was quick to learn the plan was hatched under Ike.

Billy left for England again. This time his crusade would take place in Manchester, strategically midway between London and Glasgow, where he had previously crusaded. The crusade drew an average of thirty thousand every night—even though Billy was sick the first week. Measured against any standard, but Billy's own successes, the crusade was a success. But by his standards, it was disappointing. It became etched in the team's minds like the failure at Altoona.

The team made it a model of how not to crusade. Do not campaign in a steep-staired outdoor stadium during the rainy season. Do not go where support from local churches is wavering. Do not go where the local churches try to set certain conditions and restrict the crusade. Do not hire a public relations firm from another region of the country.

When Kennedy met with the Russian leader Khrushchev that summer, Khrushchev showed the world he had no respect for him. Kennedy must have agreed because he immediately asked for more money to bolster American armed forces. Billy's dread of Communism only increased under what he considered Kennedy's blunders. Communists moved quickly if they sensed weakness. And they did. Some activity was overt. In August, the Communists built a concrete wall in Berlin to keep East Germans from fleeing to the West.

"That's bad," admitted Billy, "but it's their secret activity that worries me most."

Back in America, Billy crusaded during the fall in Philadelphia. The one-month crusade had seven interns from Columbia Presbyterian Seminary. It was the brainstorm of Lane Adams, a pastor who believed seminary students never really learned how to evangelize. So why not let them learn under the most effective evangelist in the world?

After Philadelphia, Billy attended one of the rare assemblies of the World Council of Churches in New Delhi, India. Again he was not a member, but his presence reflected the attitude of his new evangelicalism. He was not at war with the liberal clergy. They must all work together for Christ. But the movement toward "universalism" sickened him. This was an ever more popular liberal belief that all people are ultimately saved, no matter how evil they had been. To Billy, the belief went beyond being just watered-down Christianity to being totally unbiblical.

The following year, he crusaded in El Paso, Chicago, and South America. In the meantime, the world was heating up. Kennedy was stepping up American presence in South Vietnam in far-off Asia, instructing military advisers to fire back if fired upon. The press dutifully reported American advisers had first been sent there by Ike, although actually they had been sent there first by Truman.

The South American crusade, split into two separate campaigns, lasted a total of nine weeks. Billy blazed through the Catholic bastions of Colombia, Venezuela, Paraguay, Uruguay, Chile, Argentina, and Brazil. Every city was an adventure. Crowds, except for those in Venezuela, were small but intensely interested. Sometimes it seemed there were more people opposing the revival than attending.

"Think we did any good?" asked a skeptical member of the team.

"I am convinced now these people will answer the call to Christ," answered Billy. "But it will have to be done with less splash. The authorities are strongly opposed."

Sandwiched between the South American trips, Billy held a very successful crusade in Chicago in June, drawing 40,000 night after night to McCormick Place. At the finale in Soldier Field, he spoke to 116,000, one of his largest American audiences ever. Added to the taped telecast was a seven-minute appeal from Billy in the then-empty stadium. It struck a chord and thousands of letters poured in.

At the Chicago rally, twenty-seven trainees from seven different schools watched Billy and his team in action. They were bankrolled by Lowell Berry, a wealthy Californian. It seemed to be such valuable training that Robert Ferm began to structure a formal program for El Paso later that year. Billy had always toyed with the idea of a school.

"Maybe this is the form God wants my school to take," said Billy. "On-the-job training at the 'Billy Graham School of Evangelism.' "

It was also at the Chicago rally that T. W. Wilson became Billy's right-hand man. Grady's brother could get things done faster than anyone Billy ever had on the team. One incident of T. W.'s efficiency was hilarious. Billy had been sleeping in the backseat of the car while T. W. drove to Montreat. At a filling station, Billy woke up and went to the rest room while T. W. was inside paying for the gas. T. W. drove off without Billy.

Billy found out later that at least T. W. stayed true to his faith. Hours later when he discovered Billy was not in the backseat, he cried, "Oh Lord, the rapture! And I'm still here."

In August 1962, Billy's father died. For several years, Frank had suffered small strokes, each time surviving but a little weaker, a little shakier. Finally one morning in the hospital, while calmly talking to his doctor, he quietly expired. Frank was seventy-four. He had rarely attended Billy's revivals. Billy knew he didn't like to travel, and he was very self-conscious around educated folks. For many years Frank had been haunted by a revival where he had been told he was to preach the gospel. Before he died, he said Billy relieved him of that guilt. Frank had quietly amassed a fortune. The dairy had been profitable, still run by Melvin up until 1959. Then Melvin moved south to raise cattle. Frank's land began to sprout office buildings.

In September, Billy and Ruth got a letter from Stephan Tchividjian, the son of Ara Tchividjian, the man who had been their host in Switzerland. Stephan very formally asked for the hand of GiGi in marriage. He was a very mature young man studying to be a psychologist. The Grahams were not totally surprised. Stephan had shown great interest in GiGi in Switzerland.

Billy told Ruth, "Many times I have prayed for such husbands for our daughters." And he could see that Ruth was pleased, too. But who knew what GiGi thought?

The same month Billy's father died, Kennedy had announced Russian technicians were bringing missiles into Cuba just miles off the coast of America, but they were merely for Cuba's defense. Billy and a lot of other Americans were suspicious. By October, the situation in Cuba had blown into a nightmare. Russian missiles were actually aimed at the heart of America. They had nuclear warheads. Khrushchev had put one over on the young president, whom he didn't respect at all. Kennedy blockaded Cuba with warships and demanded the missiles be removed. Khrushchev answered "yes," provided America would remove its missiles from Turkey, right next to Russia. Kennedy refused. America waited anxiously for the Russian response. Finally, the Russians sheepishly removed their missiles from Cuba.

"The Communists never would have tried that with Ike," muttered Billy. Then he wondered why he hadn't thought of Nixon instead of Ike.

Billy crusaded in El Paso in November, then headed home to Little Piney Cove. By Christmas, GiGi was home from Wheaton College and Stephan Tchividjian was there, too. It seemed like no time at all before GiGi and Stephan were coordinating their wedding with Billy's crusade in France and

West Germany. They were married in May 1963.

In the second half of 1963, Billy crusaded in the Los Angeles Coliseum, drawing over 130,000 on the finale. The Billy Graham School of Evangelism was well under way. The team taught a hundred seminarians and pastors all day in classrooms. At night they all participated in the crusade. The effort was still financed by Lowell Berry, who made it clear he was committed to it for as long as Billy needed help. Berry even set up a foundation that would continue the support after Berry's death.

All of 1963 had seen racial strife. Blacks were being jailed, were marching, and were entering formerly all-white schools all over America. Billy supported the effort, but he was no more immune from criticism than any other public figure. Some scalded him for wanting to go too slow; some scalded him for wanting to go too fast. But the most shocking event of 1963 took place in November as Billy was playing golf with T. W. near Montreat.

"Somebody shot at the president in a motorcade in Dallas!" yelled someone.

"Surely not!" prayed Billy.

He and T. W. rushed to a radio station owned by BGEA.

The whole nation listened to radios and watched television as the horror trickled in. The president and Texas governor John Connally were believed to be shot. The president was rushed to a hospital. Billy went on the air. He tried to reassure the listeners. Nothing was known for sure yet.

T. W. held a note against the window of the broadcast booth: "The president is dead."

Within hours, the nation knew President Kennedy had

died at Parkland Hospital in Dallas. Lyndon Johnson was flying back with First Lady Jackie Kennedy. En route, Johnson was sworn in as president. Billy was sick. He didn't even want to think what this tragedy meant.

He was allowed to sit with the Kennedy family at the funeral. He offered his services to Lyndon Johnson. Johnson had a long history as an overbearing, arm-twisting, loudmouthed legislator from Texas. He had never expected to become president. Power brokers like Johnson just did not get elected. They had walked over too many people. Billy did not expect any rapport with Johnson.

Billy was invited to the White House within one week. He was not surprised to learn he was allowed but fifteen minutes. Johnson would use him. It was good public relations to feign a spiritual side. Yet Billy had to admit Johnson's furrowed face showed terrible strain. Billy tried to bring him the peace of God. Fifteen minutes became five hours. They swam in the White House pool. Johnson was crippled with laughter from listening to Grady's endless repertoire of jokes, delivered in his good old boy southern accent.

Billy cemented the friendship by telling the press, "Lyndon Johnson is the most qualified man ever to take on the presidency."

But the Texas billionaire H. L. Hunt soon changed that. He offered to bankroll Billy's bid for the Republican nomination in 1964. The nominating convention was only a few months away. Billy turned him down, but he was flattered. He reflected on his popularity. BGEA now got millions of letters. Billy had millions of supporters around the country. And his pavilion at the World's Fair in New York drew millions of visitors.

After a while, in his heart, he had to admit he had been turned down many times himself, and he knew when folks truly meant yes or truly meant no. He had not been firm enough with Hunt. Was the devil behind this temptation? Was Billy making Hunt raise the ante? Or maybe Billy was waiting for the offer to leak, which it soon would, so he would hear what the rest of the power moguls thought. Suddenly, he was deluged with phone calls. The callers were all negative, especially Ruth.

"Are you crazy?" she yelled over the phone.

Billy finally publicly squelched the idea. He resumed his crusades, the most notable being in Boston. This time every meeting was at the Boston Garden with a finale at Boston Commons. Billy visited the notorious Combat Zone of sleazy bars and strip-joints and purveyors of pornography. He was cheered by the sinners.

A meeting was arranged with Cardinal Cushing. The cardinal shocked Billy by urging Catholics to go to the crusade meetings. They would only become better Catholics. "I'm 100 percent for Dr. Graham," said the cardinal. "The hand of God must be upon him."

And Billy answered, "I feel much closer to Roman Catholic traditions."[2]

Billy and Ruth became grandparents. Billy was just forty-five when GiGi gave birth to the first grandchild and Ruth a mere forty-three. Ruth still had six-year-old Ned at home herself! And Franklin, the most rebellious child of all five, was only eleven. Ruth seldom traveled now.

As the 1964 election approached, Billy realized how H. L. Hunt had tempted him into making a dreadful mistake.

Johnson had enormous popularity, much of which was for his martyred predecessor, according to cynics. But for whatever reasons, Johnson steam-rollered the Republican nominee Barry Goldwater, winning the popular vote by an incredible margin of fifteen million votes! The only result worth noting was that the Deep South voted for Goldwater, stinging from Johnson's vigorous action against segregation.

Billy launched 1965 with a crusade in Hawaii. He followed with crusades in Copenhagen and Denver. Then at Lyndon Johnson's request, he visited Selma, Alabama, where there was so much racial strife that civil rights activists had been murdered. On Easter Sunday, Billy held a large integrated rally in Birmingham, where a black church had been bombed. Thirty-five thousand, half black and half white, attended.

Billy supported Lyndon Johnson's new "Great Society" programs, aimed at helping poor people. But Billy was not popular with blacks. Many demanded stronger action, not soothing influence. Why wasn't Billy in jail like Martin Luther King? Their rhetoric seemed fueled, too, by South Vietnam. America was building up its military presence quickly. It was obvious to anyone Vietnam would soon be full-scale war. Americans could not appreciate the relevance of Vietnam. Who cared what happened there?

"Blacks are sent there in an inordinate number," complained leading blacks.

In late summer, Billy had one of his dark moments. It was just days before his crusade was scheduled to begin in the Astrodome in Houston. He truly felt the Holy Spirit had deserted him. He could not preach except through the Holy Spirit. Some organizers in Houston could not understand what he meant. Surely Billy had a physical problem. Well, Houston had wonderful medical facilities.

But those closest to him knew he really meant the Holy Spirit. Two nights before the crusade was to begin, as Billy struggled to speak to a college group, he felt the Holy Spirit return. The crusade in the Astrodome was memorable, not only for that but because it was the first one a president attended. Johnson and his wife, "Lady Bird," flew over from their LBJ Ranch west of Austin for the finale.

Billy had another book published. *World Aflame* sold one-hundred-thousand copies in the first three months. The title was apt for current events in America, too. Never had America seen so much rebellion. Some blacks had tired of the American process and now spouted Communist rhetoric. College students were violently opposed to fighting in Vietnam. Billy had mixed feelings about the war himself. But he realized many young people were using their rebellion as an excuse to indulge in sex and drugs. Issues became muddled and ugly.

"The incomprehensible mixture of pigment merely denotes the confused minds and values of our day," said Billy. "Ours indeed is a sick generation in need of salvation."

Many students now openly scoffed at all authority. Critics of this new rude behavior, like Billy, seemed old-fashioned. A minority of students pillaged the offices of registrars and burned their papers. More and more students and more and more commentators on television ridiculed any American who opposed this new rebellion. To them John Wayne was nothing more than a Nazi. So was the comedian Bob Hope. The turn had been so sudden and so ugly, Billy and many other adults were flabbergasted.

When Billy went to England in 1966, he saw further proof. The deterioration of spirit had gone much further there than in America. Decay was in the very heart of the church. Leading clerics simply could no longer swallow the truths of the gospel. It just no longer met modern social needs, they claimed. And it was much too harsh for anyone to go to hell. After all, could the sinner be blamed for being corrupted by society or by his parents or by the government? Surely, all souls went to heaven.

"A merciful God will sort it all out—if there is a God," expounded one English deacon.

By any measurement of numbers, the crusade at Earls Court Arena in London was a success. Billy preached in person to over one million people in only one month. Another innovation was added: closed-circuit television to ten English cities. Sharp minds had extended his revivals before 1966 by electronics. But this state-of-the-art yielded a production almost superior to the original. A giant screen showed Billy up close, something few saw at the real event. The sound was clear and unequivocal. Billy was asked to return in 1967 and conduct another closed-circuit revival from Earls Court Arena. He should have felt very satisfied with the campaign. But he left England with a sour taste in his mouth. Universalism had raised its ugly head again—the belief that no matter what a sinner did, he would ultimately be saved.

"Our congress of evangelicals could not be more timely," Billy told his friends.

Billy had encouraged the international meeting of evangelicals but refrained from organizing it under BGEA. He did not want to control it. He did little except to suggest invitations to Fundamentalists and Pentecostals so that the congress would truly be a third Christian force in the world. He wanted an evangelical organization that would be as respected as the Catholics or the liberal Protestants' World Council of Churches.

But at the congress in Berlin, he was disappointed to hear that delegates were snubbing another delegate, the Pentecostal healer-evangelist Oral Roberts. Then he heard what Calvin Thielman, Ruth's pastor back in Montreat, had done to Roberts. Billy called Thielman and asked him to come to his room to talk privately.

"What's this I hear about you and Oral Roberts?" Billy asked Thielman.

FOURTEEN

Oral Roberts was invited, wasn't he?" answered Thielman.

"Everyone was avoiding him, Billy, so I started having lunch with him."

"God bless you, Calvin."

Billy knew Calvin had done more than that, though that would have been enough to earn God's blessing. Calvin had engineered meetings with London clerics, who had questioned Roberts's ministry of healing. And Roberts's answers had won their respect. How many times had Billy gone through the same gauntlet himself?

Back in Montreat, Anne married Danny Lotz. Bunny, fifteen, was now at Stony Brook, a boarding school in New York. So was Franklin, at fourteen. Only nine-year-old Ned was at home during the school year. Ruth was just a few years from being free to travel with Billy during the school year, although summers would be occupied with children for many years to come.

Billy went to Vietnam for Christmas. He preached twenty-five times, often combining talents with Bob Hope. Vietnam was far worse than he had thought. The situation was profoundly depressing. Unless America threw its full might into the war, he saw no way to win and no way to get out. After he said that very thing in a press conference, he was told by American officials that comments like his were the very thing that broke the spirit of our fighting men and women. So the next day, he issued an optimistic assessment. But he left, convinced Vietnam was the most unfortunate foreign venture in America's long history. He knew Communism was unadulterated godless evil, but he began to doubt it was a monolithic monster trying to take over the world. And it began to disappear more and more from his sermons. He began aiming at the problems of ordinary individuals.

In his citywide crusades, now trimmed to a Sunday-to-Sunday eight days, he started each sermon behind the pulpit, which had clocks seen only by him and guests on the platform. He always knew exactly how much time he had remaining before he invited people to the altar. His preaching had fallen into a very successful format. In his experience, people suffered from four maladies: emptiness, loneliness, guilt, and fear of death. Unless he was aiming at a specific audience like teenagers and how they could enlist Christ to fight sexual temptation, he would tackle one of those main four human miseries.

Pop-pop-pop. He would begin by describing their innermost feelings of misery, straying away from the pulpit, hammering points with exaggerated gestures:

> *You're empty! You're mixed up! You're confused! Life has no meaning. Many of you without money think money*

*will make you happy. Many of you have money and
you are not happy.*

Then he would paint an even grimmer picture. The pace
was breathless:

*The time of your death is not known to you. Some of
you may die tonight. Some may die tomorrow. We all
die. Alone. Are you ready to die tonight? Tomorrow?
Are you ready for the eternal tomb of sinners?*

Then he would hammer out the good news. His voice
was full of joy and hope:

*There was a God who became a man. The Godman.
Christ! He came to earth to die for your sins. All of you!
The ground is level at the foot of the cross!*

But salvation required a commitment. There was little
time to waste. Who knew what could happen tomorrow?
Even tonight? His voice was urgent again:

*This may be the hour for which you were born. Tonight
may determine your eternal destiny. You can come to
Christ and turn your whole life around. You can save
your soul for eternity. You can come to the cross. Or you
can walk away from the cross. You can accept God. Or
you can separate from God. The choice is yours!*

And the commitment had to be public. The Bible said so.
Standing in public made the commitment stronger:

All you have to do to earn eternal salvation is to con-fess with your mouth before the world, "Jesus, I am a sinner" and repent, "I'll sin no more," and declare your faith "Jesus is Lord." And through God's grace Christ will come into your heart! Then follow Christ through the fellowship of the church.

Then Billy called them forward.

Come forward, please. There's a man out there who is not sure. Come forward. A woman out there is trying to decide. Come forward now.

Billy was always very uneasy during the call to the altar. But as dozens of lost souls started to come forward for salvation, he was overwhelmed by his gift. He was so unworthy. He would plant his chin in his right hand, suddenly very self-conscious, reminding himself they were responding to the Holy Spirit, not Billy Graham. And yet when they arrived, he had to acknowledge them. He tried to make eye contact with every one of them. Who could know if that might make their conversion just a little stronger? They were babes. They had to be encouraged in every way.

He said the "sinner's prayer" with them:

Oh God, I am a sinner. I'm sorry for my sins. I'm will-ing to turn from my sins. I receive Christ as my Savior. I confess Him as my Lord. From this moment on, I want to follow Him and serve Him in the fellowship of the church. In Christ's name, Amen.[1]

Then counselors took them under their wings.

The year 1967 was the first year Billy really cut back. His schedule was limited to the Earls Court follow-up and eight-day crusades in Puerto Rico, Winnipeg, Kansas City, and Tokyo. He would turn forty-nine. He already had suffered kidney stones, hypertension, prostate surgery, an edema from stress, and many minor ailments.

He spent a lot of time with Lyndon Johnson. Two dozen times he had been a guest at Camp David, the White House, or the LBJ Ranch. The war was crushing Johnson. He had attained the pinnacle, and he had the legislative skills to move the nation any direction he wanted. But the failure of the war drained him. He was now very unpopular, almost impotent. He took every American death in the war personally. And like Lincoln, he suffered from a premonition he would die young.

"The Johnson men do not live long," confided Johnson. He asked Billy more and more about his salvation. In one very dark mood, he told Billy he wanted him to preach at his funeral. "Say something nice about me," he muttered.

By spring 1967, Johnson confided to Billy he probably would not run for reelection. That same year, Richard Nixon's mother died, and Billy spoke at her funeral. She had always doted on Billy. If Billy looked too thin on television, she would call and in a worried voice order him to eat better. Nixon broke down at the funeral and sobbed on Billy's shoulder. Later Nixon invited Billy to Florida. He admitted to Billy he might run for president again. Should he or shouldn't he? Billy said if he didn't, he would always regret it.

For 1968, Billy had crusades scheduled for Australia, Portland, Pittsburgh, and San Antonio. While he was in

Australia, the world turned topsy-turvy. Johnson announced he would not run again. Days later, Martin Luther King was killed by a sniper. Things did not improve after Billy returned. The virtual shoo-in for the Democratic nomination, Robert Kennedy, was assassinated in Los Angeles—just as his brother John had been assassinated five years earlier in Dallas.

Billy was heartsick at what was happening in America. He said, "America is going through its greatest crisis since the Civil War."[2]

Even Little Piney Cove was a grim reminder of how sick America had become. Although Ned was the only child still at home, life was more complicated there now. Billy was getting too many death threats. The assassinations proved the threats were all too real. Now an eleven-foot fence had to be constructed around the home at Little Piney Cove. Any approaching driver had to radio the house. Then an electronically controlled gate would open. Even at that, any visitor was greeted by bristling German shepherds, trained to explode in a split second. The protection was very depressing, even though the Grahams had been vulnerable so many years.

Billy intended to stay away from the nomination and election processes for president in 1968, but he was kidding only himself. At the Portland crusade just before the Republican convention, he introduced Julie and Tricia, the daughters of Richard and Pat Nixon. At the convention, he led the delegates in prayer after Richard Nixon delivered his acceptance speech. That night he was even privy to the selection of Nixon's vice presidential candidate. About twenty powerful Republicans bantered back and forth hour after hour. Finally, Billy left the meeting before a choice was made.

"They chose Spiro Agnew?" Billy said in surprise the next day. "I don't think Nixon even knows him." Later Billy heard Strom Thurmond had insisted on Agnew. But Billy had been in the meeting and knew that wasn't true at all. Oh, politics was so very complicated.

At the September crusade in Pittsburgh just before the election, he gave Nixon a boost by allowing him to sit prominently in the V.I.P. guest section. That particular revival meeting was televised nationally. Nixon made a great show of visiting Billy's aging mother, Morrow, in Charlotte. Nixon's daughter Julie visited Ruth in Montreat. And four days before the election in November, Billy admitted to the press that on his absentee ballot he had voted for Richard Nixon.

Nixon squeaked out the narrowest of victories over Hubert Humphrey. The racist demagogue George Wallace ran as a third-party candidate. The next morning, Billy met Nixon for breakfast. Nixon asked him to lead them in prayer that very moment for the great job ahead.

"Billy, I want you to lead us in prayer. We want to rededicate our lives."[3]

Nixon wanted to give Billy ten minutes for a prayer at the inauguration in January, but Billy insisted the time be shared with other faiths. But there was little doubt Nixon had special regard for Billy. Nixon was the first president to institute a regular White House church service on Sunday morning, and he asked Billy to line up preachers for the service. Billy was only too happy to boost the show of faith. He scheduled plenty of evangelicals, but he also invited Catholic clerics and mainline Protestant pastors.

Of course, Billy preached the first service in the East

Room of the White House. But he insisted, "I want to preach only once a year."

In March 1969, Billy was called to Walter Reed Hospital in Washington, D.C. Ike was in bed, ghostly white with nothing left but a trace of the famous grin. He had been there for almost a year, dying. He had asked for Billy. They talked about eternity. Four days later, Ike died.

It seemed an older era died with the old peacemaker. Race and Vietnam were the burning issues in America now. And Billy's positions did not change. He continued to talk to all parties in the South to cool off tempers whenever he could. He continued to give spiritual support to American troops in Vietnam and outwardly act optimistic about the war's outcome. He also continued his crusades during the Nixon presidency, talking with Nixon occasionally and with Nixon's chief of staff, H. R. Haldeman, weekly.

His special status with Nixon's White House thrilled him and bothered him at the same time. God forgive him if he was being used. It seemed Nixon genuinely respected him and used him for a sounding board. It seemed that he and Nixon were truly friends. And, of course, the friendship occasionally took the form of actions.

He once conveyed Nixon's concern about Israeli military ambitions to Billy's friend Golda Meir, who was now the prime minister of Israel. Another time Billy confided to Nixon that ex-President Johnson wanted to be part of the Apollo 11 festivities after Neil Armstrong walked on the moon. Nixon saw that it was done. Yet another time, Billy conveyed to Nixon Indira Gandhi's criteria for a good ambassador to India, resulting in the appointment of Patrick Moynihan. On the other hand, Nixon spoke at Billy's crusade in Knoxville. This was a tremendous triumph in Billy's eyes. How important it was to have the president openly espouse faith.

"If only I could get Nixon to call for a national day of repentance like Lincoln had!" cried Billy.

On the home front in 1969, Bunny married Ted Dienert, the son of the advertising executive who had pestered Billy into starting *Hour of Decision* so many years ago. All three daughters were now married, every one by the age of eighteen. Franklin had returned home from Stony Brook in New York to finish high school in a local public school. Determined not to be a "preacher boy," he flaunted vices. He smoked cigarettes, drank alcohol, and topped his image with long hair. He rode a motorcycle and terrorized young Ned.

And Ruth warred with Franklin. One time when he overslept, she dumped his ashtray full of cigarette butts on his head. Several times she decided to win him over by showing him what a good sport she was. She hopped on his motorcycle and ran it over an embankment. Another time she rode it into a lake. The last time a split-rail fence stopped her. Ruth was never the socialite she appeared to be. She was much more at home clubbing a rattlesnake on the mountain behind Little Piney Cove than clubbing a golf ball. Of course, Billy had always known she marched to a different drummer. And he knew about the dreadful things she had endured as a child.

Billy's brothers and sisters were involved in Billy's enterprises, too. His sister Jean was married to one of BGEA's most able preachers, Leighton Ford. His sister Catherine was married to Samuel McElroy, who worked in BGEA's Charlotte office. Melvin was never officially with BGEA, but he did take the platform in the crusade at Anaheim. He told the crowd how intimidated he had been in Billy's shadow, but now he, too, had a responsibility to tell others about Jesus. And he wasn't going to stop speaking when he returned to North Carolina.

In October 1971, Charlotte held a Billy Graham Day. When first approached by the president of the Chamber of Commerce, Billy resisted. But the Chamber of Commerce played an ace in the hole. Richard Nixon liked the idea. Billy couldn't refuse the president of the United States. Nixon was superb at Billy Graham Day, speaking warmly about Billy without notes. Later, Billy was deluged with telegrams from notables like Ronald Reagan, Jimmy Stewart, Bob Hope, and Arnold Palmer. Among the guests was proud, silver-haired Morrow Graham, who still lived in the family home, surrounded not by cows and green fields but sprawling franchises and office buildings.

Ruth was skeptical. "Isn't Nixon using you?"

"I get as good as I give."

Billy wasn't so naive he didn't realize Nixon was running for president again. But the truth was he had always curried favor with the White House to help his ministry. Besides, he liked Nixon. Billy saw a loose side of Nixon few people ever saw. Part of it was because of irrepressible Grady Wilson. When Grady golfed with Billy and the president, Nixon would needle Grady as "Greedy Grady" because plump Grady was so deceptively good at golf. Nixon would pat Grady's fat belly and say, "That tummy's got to come down." Or he would grab Grady's arm and crack, "Pray for me, I'm a backslider."[4]

Still, at the end of 1971, Billy resolved he must not get involved in the presidential election of 1972 as he had in

1968. Yet Nixon pointedly told him he needed help in Pennsylvania, Ohio, Illinois, and New York. And Billy agonized: Why not help Nixon? What other president had the vision to try to open up Red China?

Even reticent Ruth was thrilled. "Part of my heart is still in China. Could you ask Nixon to take a religious correspondent with him on his momentous visit to Red China?"

Billy did manage to avoid the national conventions that summer. The selection of ultraliberal George McGovern to run against Nixon seemed a disastrous choice for Democrats. As if to seal the results of the election, a very depressed Lyndon Johnson confided to Billy he was appalled at the choice. This was one election that needn't worry Billy. His good friend Nixon would be reelected for sure. And he was.

The day after Christmas 1972, Harry Truman died—at the age of eighty-eight. He had gotten crustier every year. Some of his comments about Billy had not been kind. But Billy did not bear a grudge. Truman had accorded Billy a rare privilege. And Billy had in fact bungled his White House visit. It had been a valuable lesson that served him well. It would only be his devil-driven pride that craved approval from Truman at long last. The approval never came.

The new year of 1973 was busy. Nixon had launched a savage bombing campaign in Vietnam in December. Billy was heartsick. He thought a cease-fire was imminent. Would they ever extract themselves from that lost cause? Then his old friend Lyndon Johnson died of a heart attack. As promised, Billy spoke at the funeral in Texas.

In the second week of Nixon's new term, the war ceased! Praise the Lord. Billy felt like crowing. "See, I told you he could do it." But he didn't like to see Americans running from Vietnam like whipped dogs with their tails between their legs. It would take a long time to live down that war. But no one wins every battle. Certainly not Israel—when they abandoned God.

"Why is America any different?" he wondered. And Billy realized how the shame of Vietnam had chipped away at his patriotism and his confidence in America. But somehow he was closer to God. Maybe that was the lesson of Vietnam.

Billy finally held a meeting in South Africa. For years, he had refused to hold a revival in South Africa unless all South Africans were allowed to attend in unrestricted seating. The government acquiesced in 1973. The crowd of forty-five thousand at Durban's Kings Park was completely integrated. South African blacks were crying with joy. They hailed Billy's influence. Ironically, American blacks lambasted him for not taking stronger action in America.

Two months later, he campaigned in South Korea. Korea was 10 percent Christian, and his host committee was wildly optimistic. They were going to stage the meetings on a former air strip, now called People's Plaza, a ribbon of concrete that stretched for one mile. But apprehensions about over-reaching soon disappeared. The first service drew five hundred thousand South Koreans! As always, Billy's short, punchy sentences were ideal for translation. And to make the event attain perfection, the translator, a South Korean trained at Bob Jones University, was a magnificent preacher himself.

By the finale, expectations for a huge turnout were extremely high. But the crowd exceeded those expectations. Never had there been a crowd like this for a religious service. Its respectful silence made the attendance of 1,100,000 even harder to believe. In five days, Billy had preached to 3 million South Koreans.

"This crusade is truly the work of God," marveled Billy.

That summer of 1973, congressional hearings in Washington, D. C., began to heat up on what appeared to be only a trivial crime. During the previous presidential campaign, thugs had broken into the Democratic National Committee's headquarters at the Watergate Apartments. It soon became known Nixon's reelection committee had something to do with it. Billy had to admit that was more than stupid; it was very dishonest. Still, any group could have a few renegades, reasoned Billy. The hearings were really just an opportunity for Democrats to embarrass Republicans. Surely Nixon had nothing to do with what was now called simply "Watergate." He had said so publicly.

"It will all blow over," said Billy to Ruth.

In June, one of Nixon's aides said Nixon learned about the break-in and covered it up. Surely, thought Billy, the aide was lying to get leniency. In July, the Watergate hearings exposed the fact that all conversations in the Oval Office were taped by Nixon. The committee wanted those tapes. Nixon refused. Billy wasn't worried about his own conversations with Nixon. Few had been in the Oval Office. Besides, he could understand that Nixon wanted tapes to write his memoirs as accurately and as honestly as possible. The tapes were never intended to be released.

"And even if they are now released, so what?" shrugged Billy.

FIFTEEN

A s the summer wore on, the Watergate committee was not able to get the tapes. But the identity of those involved in the break-in at the Watergate Apartments climbed higher and higher in Nixon's administration. Aides that Billy had talked to were involved. He had always felt Nixon's aides were transparent the way they tried to use him. This incident just proved they were dishonorable.

"It certainly does not involve Richard Nixon," Billy assured himself, "or even H. R. Haldeman." They could be accused of bad judgment in picking staff.

The summer of 1973 was a sad, dismal one for the Grahams. In August, Nelson Bell, eighty and diabetic, passed away. He was buried in Swannanoa. Ruth's mother, Virginia, clung to life, her voice gone from a stroke. In the fall, Nixon's vice president, Spiro Agnew, resigned. His resignation had nothing to do with Watergate. It seemed almost providential the way Nixon's administration, having stopped the war in

Vietnam and opened up Red China, was disintegrating and passing on into history.

Billy and other Nixon friends advised him to make a complete confession. It wasn't too late. In April 1974, Nixon petulantly released transcripts of selected tapes and claimed loudly to the nation he was innocent of any wrong-doing. Friends told Billy the transcripts were peppered with profanity.

"Yes," admitted Billy, "I know Nixon says 'hell' and 'damn' when he's agitated, but he always apologizes for using them."

After his Phoenix campaign in May, Billy finally sat down to read the transcripts of the Oval Office tapes. Astonishment turned to horror. Billy cried. He threw up. What a fool he had been. The Nixon on the tapes was a man he didn't know. Nixon was foul, cynical, hateful. Billy looked into his own heart and, like John Wesley, he saw hell. He prayed several days, then composed a watered-down press release deploring the moral tone of the White House.

"I won't be the one to destroy Richard Nixon," he told himself. "He's doing that to himself."

On August 9, 1974, Nixon resigned. The Watergate committee had found indisputable proof on the tapes that Nixon endorsed the cover-up. Billy tried to call him to console him, but Nixon would not take his calls. Within one month, President Gerald Ford pardoned Nixon of all crimes, defending his pardon by saying a lengthy trial would bring the government to a halt. It was in the national interest to get Watergate behind us. Billy was very grateful Nixon would not be flogged any more in public.

Some critics wanted to tar and feather Billy with Nixon, inferring he was an insider. The irony was that Billy had been closer to President Johnson. Johnson invited him to the White House twenty-three times, five of those for overnight. Billy's visits to Nixon in the White House had been fewer. Johnson had Billy to Camp David twice; Nixon had Billy there once. And Johnson had invited Billy to the LBJ Ranch, too. The truth was that Billy knew more of the inner workings of Johnson's White House than Nixon's. But as usual, Billy ignored slander and innuendoes.

In October, Billy crusaded in South America. Ruth took the opportunity to visit GiGi and the grandchildren. In Brazil, Billy got a phone call from GiGi. Ruth was in the hospital!

"What happened?" he cried.

"She rigged up a pipe slide for the children," explained GiGi. Billy knew a pipe slide was a short section of pipe on a wire strung at a steep angle between two trees. The slider gripped the pipe and careened down the wire. Did it seem out of character for the Ruth he knew? Not at all. "She tried it first to make sure it was safe for the children," continued GiGi. *Well, thank God for that,* thought Billy. "It wasn't safe," added GiGi. "The wire broke and she fell fifteen feet."

"Anything broken?"

"Broken heel, cracked rib, and crushed vertebra," said GiGi sadly.

"How is she taking it? Let me talk to her."

"I'm sorry. She also has a concussion." GiGi hesitated. "She's in a coma."

Oh God, prayed Billy, *don't take Ruth yet.* How could he continue without her?

Ruth regained consciousness, but her memory was a shambles. *What else can go wrong?* thought Billy. As if he were being punished for his lack of trust, Ruth's mother died. But of course he knew he had nothing to do with it. Virginia Bell was buried in Swannanoa next to Nelson. Ruth could barely stand on crutches at the funeral. Billy felt so sad for Ruth. Here she was, trying to recover from her foolishness, and now she had lost both parents. Thank God, at least she didn't have to worry about Franklin. That summer in Switzerland and the Holy Land, the Lord had become real to Franklin. He had accepted Jesus as his Lord. Billy knew it was real, too. Praise the Lord. In fear of having a second Franklin to deal with, Billy and Ruth had sent Ned to a school in England, where discipline was very severe. They had realized their mistake. Ned was no problem. Now he was back at Stony Brook. *Good times lay ahead for all of us*, thought Billy—*if Ruth gets her memory back.*

Over the weeks, Ruth recovered her memory. But her hip was deteriorating, possibly from the accident. Hip surgery loomed somewhere in her future, said the doctors.

Billy backed away from the White House now. Never again would he delude himself into being unofficial chaplain of the White House, thinking he was advancing the gospel, but instead actually just being used as a small political pawn. In his darker moments, he wondered if Lyndon Johnson had used him.

"Maybe even Ike used me," he speculated in his darkest moments.

He visited with President Gerald Ford and prayed with him. Ford was congenial but conveyed no hint of wanting a close relationship, as Nixon and Johnson had done. Billy invited Ford to a crusade, as he had invited every president since Truman in 1952. Ford declined. Billy continued to crusade and lightly manage BGEA.

BGEA had two major successes in 1975 away from the crusade circuit. World Wide Pictures made its most professional film, *The Hiding Place*, about the heroic ten Boom family of Holland. They hid Jews and other refugees during World War II at a heavy price: imprisonment in Nazi death camps. The lone survivor of the family, spunky eighty-three-year-old Corrie ten Boom, attended the premiere. Corrie was a prime example of an itinerant evangelist, still living out of a suitcase, preaching the gospel.

Billy had enormous admiration for her. "I've never been tested like she has," he admitted to himself.

For a while that fall, Billy's book called *Angels* became the best-selling nonfiction hardcover. Billy wrote it because he could hardly believe there was no modern book on such a heavenly creation as angels. It was a symptom of the times that people were losing their belief in angels. Billy intended to do something about it. He was not interested in commercial success. He was motivated only by need.

In summer 1976, Ford expressed interest in speaking at Billy's crusade in Michigan. Billy was disappointed that the president only showed interest in speaking at a crusade in an election year; the interest was motivated by politics. Billy politely refused to let him speak, inviting Ford to sit in his V.I.P. section instead, and he added that he would extend an invitation to Ford's opponent, Georgia governor Jimmy Carter. Ford declined.

Billy had known Jimmy Carter for many years. Carter was a devout evangelical Christian. In 1966, Carter had chaired a small crusade built around showing Billy's film *The Restless Ones*. Carter had wholeheartedly accepted Billy's mandate that the audiences be integrated. After each showing of the film, Carter himself explained the gospel and invited the audience to the altar. In 1973, Carter chaired the full-fledged crusade in Atlanta and invited Billy for an overnight stay at the governor's mansion.

Billy felt very warm toward Jimmy Carter. But he also honestly doubted Carter was up to the job as president. Carter was a graduate of the naval academy. So he had both military experience and executive experience. And yet there was an appeasing attitude in Carter that worried Billy. Enemies of America were so quick to jump on weakness. And the reporters were quick to jump on Billy's doubts.

Carter had a temper, snapping that Billy went "around telling people how to live their lives." Carter's son Jeff accused Billy of having a mail-order degree.[1]

Billy tried to smooth it over by writing Jimmy's wife, Rosalyn, a letter. And when Carter was elected, Billy was quick to announce his full support for the new president. But Billy did not attend the inauguration, the first one he had missed in twenty years. Although he was a guest at the White House within a month, Billy's relationship with Carter was congenial but cool, much as it had been with Ford. Carter almost immediately pardoned all those who had evaded the draft during the war in Vietnam. That seemed to be a new political tool: Act immediately on anything that is going to be extremely unpopular in the hope that people will forget it before the next election.

But Billy reflected, "That didn't work very well for Gerald Ford, did it?"

In March, while crusading in Las Vegas, Billy got a shock. Grady Wilson, who over the years had ballooned to 235 pounds, suffered a massive heart attack back in North Carolina. Billy rushed east. At the hospital, the doctor said no one could visit Grady in intensive care.

"Doctor," said Billy calmly, "I'm going into Grady's room, and I'm going in now." And he entered the room to pray at Grady's side. Of all the team members, Grady was closest to Billy. He was Billy's sidekick and the one who kicked him in the seat of the pants when his nose was too high in the air.

Grady recovered, and Billy soon had little time to think about anything but his own reputation. In spring 1977, the Charlotte newspaper, the *Observer*, ran a very detailed series on the financial structure of BGEA. Billy had fed them information himself, right on the porch of Little Piney Cove. The BGEA was a large organization to be sure, but it was clean. Every year the organization spent as much money as it collected. And collections were low-key, never threatening or hysterical pandering or promising great prosperity.

BGEA had several hundred employees in Minneapolis. Its two buildings had modest histories. One was a three-story office building bought many years ago from an oil company. Its neighbor was once a parking garage. The board of directors had over twenty members, both inside and outside the BGEA. The secret to BGEA's financial integrity was that all decisions had to be approved by an executive committee made up of outside directors who did not receive payments from BGEA. The outside directors were all seasoned executives of other companies. As far back as 1960, the executive committee had set up a trust for all the royalties from Billy's books—at the time a mere two books, but by 1977, six books with sales in the millions of copies. A bank administered the trust, directing money to BGEA or other charities.

Like any institution, BGEA had critics. Some complained about the generous pension plans for workers in BGEA. Some complained about the annuities solicited by BGEA. But Billy had been extra cautious even with those. The principal behind the annuity was always completely protected during the lifetime of the contributor. So in the unlikely case BGEA ever went bankrupt, the annuity contributors would get every nickel of the principal back. And BGEA refused to invest in public stocks, so as not to appear to endorse any corporation or product.

As Billy finished reading the final installment of the series, he sighed. "The Charlotte *Observer* concluded BGEA is squeaky clean and had the decency to say so."

But as careful as Billy had been with his financial dealings and disclosing them, in summer 1977, the *Observer* screamed betrayal and hypocrisy. The investigative reporters who wrote the series for the *Observer* discovered there was another organization connected with Billy that did not spend all the money it collected but had amassed over twenty million dollars—and that was invested heavily in public stock! The World Evangelism and Christian Education Fund (WECEF) was incorporated in Dallas. Nine of its eleven board members were also board members of BGEA. The other two were Ruth and her brother Clayton!

"Why didn't they ask me about that before they attacked me in their paper?" lamented Billy. "Now it looks like I was hiding something."

Billy now had to devote much time to defending himself.

He had to explain on the *Hour of Decision* that WECEF was a separate organization set up to promote three missions. It was to establish in Asheville a training center for laymen. Secondly, it was to start a training center for evangelism connected with Wheaton College. Thirdly, it funded the youth programs: Campus Crusade, the Fellowship of Christian Athletes, and Young Life. Why did WECEF have such a surplus of money? Because the first two missions would require such funds when construction actually started. And WECEF was no secret. Billy had announced its creation in Minneapolis in 1970.

Later Billy remembered that as recently as 1976, he had discussed it candidly with a reporter from another newspaper in the same chain that owned the *Observer*! The reporter had not used the material, but he had taped the conversation. When the *Observer* was informed of this and still refused to retract their accusations, Billy managed to get the tape released to the Associated Press. They printed the truth about the situation, and many editorials scolded the *Observer* for deliberately not setting the record straight.

"But many Americans will remember only the accusation," lamented Billy.

He thought he had been careful with money matters, but he realized now he had to be even more careful. All evangelical organizations had to be more careful. He immediately set about to organize a council that would hold evangelical organizations accountable for the way they handled money. It was time to put a stop to the growing image of money-grubbing evangelicals. Evangelicals had a high profile now on television, as cable channels proliferated.

Later in 1977, Billy met with Alex Haraszti, an evangelical

surgeon in Atlanta. Haraszti was a naturalized American who had immigrated from Hungary to escape Communism.

Haraszti asked, "How would you like to hold a full-fledged crusade in Hungary?"

"A crusade for Christ in a Communist country? What a question. Of course I would!"

Haraszti explained that America had two things Hungary wanted. Since the end of World War II, the American army had held Hungary's most precious religious symbol, the Crown of St. Stephen, Hungary's patron saint. America refused to return it, claiming Hungary's current government was not legitimate, no more than a puppet controlled by the Russians. And secondly, the current government in Hungary wanted "most-favored-nation" trade status with America.

"But how can we deliver these things?" asked Billy nervously. "Those things can only be obtained at the highest level of government." Was Haraszti going to ask Billy to use his influence with Jimmy Carter?

"Leave it to me," said Haraszti.

Haraszti launched his plan, as intricate as an espionage thriller, to get Billy's crusade into Hungary. By late 1977, Billy opened his crusade in a church in Budapest. The few hundred Hungarians there were not only nervous, they were mildly hostile. Why was this happening? But, as always, Billy's preaching won their hearts. The hostility turned into anticipation, then love. By the end of the ten days, he had preached several times, once to a crowd of thirty thousand. He also met with Jewish leaders and government officials.

The Hungarian triumph seemed to break down the barriers to the eastern European countries. Apparently the word spread at the highest levels. Billy was not dangerous. He might even satiate the populace's hunger for God, which never seemed to go away. The following year Billy preached in Poland.

In 1979, Billy finally saw the formation of the organization called the Evangelical Council for Financial Accountability (ECFA). Membership in ECFA would be voluntary. But he knew one organization that would join and would strictly adhere to its guidelines: BGEA.

The Carter years had been hard for Billy to watch. Here was a president openly devout but ineptly applying Christian principles to world affairs. Carter was being bludgeoned by nominal Christians and non-Christians alike, only too happy to exploit his inappropriate Sermon-on-the-Mount meekness. In 1979, Iran did the unthinkable. Thugs stormed the American embassy, violating a time-honored tradition everywhere in the world of protecting official foreign representatives. The Iranians taunted the sixty-three American hostages month after month.

"It's heartbreaking," said Billy, "to see Carter grope powerlessly for a solution."

The solution came in January 1981. The very day Ronald Reagan was inaugurated as the new president, the hostages were released. Reagan had promised immediate military action against Iran if they were not released. Billy knew, as everyone seemed to sense, that Reagan was not posturing. He had known Reagan for over twenty-five years. Reagan was resolute but disarmingly affable. He was a master of communication. He was totally honest. He had visions of what the world was about. He delegated authority.

A friend told Billy, "You know, in many ways, Reagan is just like you, Billy."

Later that year, Billy went to Red China with Ruth, her brother Clayton, and her sisters, Rosa and Virgina. They visited the old family mission in Tsingkiang. Ruth had tried to arrange the trip for years. The trip had finally been expedited by none other than Richard Nixon, who had remained a friend of Billy's. They had reconciled several months after Nixon's resignation. The China trip was far more than a trip into nostalgia. Billy had been briefed on which officials he had to convince if he ever hoped to crusade in China. And Billy met with them, patiently explaining that Christians were good citizens, illustrating with Romans 13 that the Bible instructed Christians to obey authorities. The Bible told Christians never to get drunk and never to steal. Billy took the officials right through the Ten Commandments on up to the pinnacle of moral perfection, the Sermon on the Mount. Now Billy would just have to go home and wait for God's will to be done.

In Charlotte, Billy's mother was now bedridden, struck down by a series of strokes. Many times she quoted to Billy the verses from Second Timothy that she and Franklin Graham had prayed in Billy's behalf for many years: "Do your best to present yourself to God as one approved, a workman who does not need to be ashamed and who correctly handles the word of truth." His mother still prayed for him. It was a great comfort to Billy to know that such a good heart was constantly appealing to God in his behalf.

At first his mother dreaded being helpless and looking frayed and confused. But she said she realized Satan was tempting her to complain. Finally, she comforted herself with Psalm 34: "The angel of the LORD encamps around those who fear him, and he delivers them." And more than once she described angelic beings around her bed. In August 1981, Morrow Graham, nearly ninety years old, passed away.

"I never felt more mortal," said Billy, now sixty-two. Was he, too, winding down at long last? What was left for him to accomplish?

SIXTEEN

B ut it was just one of Billy's dark moments.
   Doors kept opening. . . .

Billy met with the Pope for the first time. John Paul II seemed to have a special interest in Billy. In 1978, Billy had established a real rapport with the Catholic clerics in Poland. Word must have filtered back to the Pope, who was from Poland, that Billy was a serious advocate for Christ, speaking with much moral authority. They discussed relations among the great Christian movements, the rise of evangelicalism, and how Christians should respond to moral issues.

"He was so down-to-earth, I forgot he was the Pope," gushed Billy afterward.[1]

Billy felt the onset of the third great goal of his life. The first had been his commitment to preach the gospel of Jesus Christ, the second to the elimination of racial injustice, and the third to world peace. And world peace could never be attained without dealing with Communism. Billy's most immediate goal was to crusade into the very center of Communism. He refused to think of it as having a heart, only a center.

"To reach the center—Russia—would be a real blow for Christ," he prayed.

Once again it was the uncanny shrewdness of Alex Haraszti that brought it about. Who else could spar with a Machiavellian heavyweight like the Russian ambassador Drobynin? Certainly Billy couldn't. He didn't even try but deferred to Haraszti at every turn. The result was the arrival of Billy in Moscow in May 1982—to preach the gospel of Jesus Christ!

Jumpy diplomats at the American State Department urged him privately not to go, hinting President Reagan was very much against it. Newspapers reported that Reagan was opposed. The Sunday before Billy was to leave, he was invited to lunch with Vice President George Bush. After Billy's arrival, the Reagans showed up. The president pulled him aside, assuring Billy he must go to Russia.

In Moscow, after a series of changes imposed by very thin-skinned Communists who were determined that Billy would not draw a large crowd of Russians, he preached at a church, unannounced, very early on a Sunday morning. The sermon still drew an audience of one thousand. The Communists intercepted others trying to get there and kept them behind barricades several blocks away. But Billy was delighted.

"We've made a real start for Christ," he told Haraszti.

Several people used the occasion to make public protests of Communist injustice. Billy brushed them off. He had to restrain himself from sympathizing publicly, or he would never be allowed to return. Patience was always one of his virtues. And he had preached to more people face-to-face than anyone in history, so perhaps he knew a thing or two about planting mustard seeds.

The secular press knew nothing of mustard seeds and magnified every gaffe Billy made in Russia. When Billy spoke of religious freedom in Russia in the hope it would come about, the press chided him for being a backward rube, a dupe of the Russians. Billy just told himself the attacks were not personal. He was on the receiving end of a very hostile press that, since Watergate, had grown more and more abusive to every public figure.

For a long time, Billy had wanted a world conference for evangelicals who were really out there preaching to sinners. Earlier congresses at Berlin and Lausanne dealt with matters far more abstract than being heckled on a street corner. Now he wanted a conference that instructed evangelists on how to compose sermons, how to draw crowds, how to raise money, how to use videos, and every other aspect of day-to-day evangelizing. The conference held in Amsterdam in 1983 was called the International Conference for Itinerant Evangelists, or ICIE. It drew nearly four thousand preachers from one hundred countries. Their tales were both encouraging and heart-breaking. One Kenyan had seen only 130 people converted in ten years. That was too typical. And some preachers were so poor, they collected empty plastic cups and trays at the conference to take back with them. They couldn't bear to see such wonderful utensils wasted.

"This conference is surely one of the best ideas the Lord ever gave me," said Billy.

During the early 1980s, Billy held crusades in Canada, Japan, Mexico, and England as well as Anaheim, Anchorage, Baltimore, Boston, Boise, Chapel Hill, Fort Lauderdale, Hartford, Houston, Oklahoma City, Orlando, San Jose, Spokane, and Tacoma. He never minimized the effects of any of these efforts, his main calling. But one crusade was very special to him. In September 1984, Billy finally got his first full-fledged crusade in Russia.

Alex Haraszti had relentlessly pursued his goal to open up Russia. Billy was allowed to preach over twelve days in four cities: Moscow, Leningrad, Novosibirsk, and Tallinin in Estonia. If the trip were not momentous enough for Billy, there was an added benchmark. His son, Franklin, newly ordained, preached with him. Another heartening aspect of the trip was the outspoken desire of fledgling Russian clerics to learn how to preach.

In 1986, Amsterdam again hosted the International Congress of Itinerant Evangelists. This time, ICIE drew over nine thousand evangelists, many brought there at the expense of BGEA. Some stories were coming back about the results of the previous conference. Some evangelists were having staggering successes now. The Kenyan who had seen only 130 converts in ten years was now seeing nearly 10,000 come to Christ each year!

The ICIE also hatched a plan of staggering proportions. With transmission of television now possible by communication satellites circling the globe, a program could be beamed to many portable receiving stations all around the world—even in remote areas, as long as they could find a large enough audience to justify it. They began to plan an enormous network of receiving stations radiating from Billy's live London crusade in English and from his live Latin American crusade in English/Spanish. They would call it "Mission World."

In 1986, Billy also held a Greater Washington, D.C., Crusade, the first one in which he rigorously enlisted help from black churches from the outset. Other crusades followed in Columbia, South Carolina, Denver, Tallahassee, and abroad in France and Helsinki. A crusade in China was now deemed possible. There just seemed to be no stopping evangelistic opportunities.

And yet, 1987 was a year of infamy for American evangelists. Billy felt helpless as he watched evangelism tainted by immorality, dishonesty, and bizarre behavior. The first blow came when his old friend Oral Roberts solicited funds on television by saying that God told him he would be taken to heaven if several million dollars were not raised for Oral's medical school in Tulsa. The second blow came when Jimmy Bakker of PTL (Praise the Lord) Ministries was scandalized when it became known he paid hush money to a church secretary with whom he had an affair. PTL, already very shaky financially, was revealed as a fiasco, promising contributors accommodations at their resort, Heritage USA—accommodations that didn't exist. Bakker and his wife were drawing annual salaries and bonuses totaling over one million dollars as the PTL ministry was going bankrupt. The third blow came when popular televangelist Jimmy Swaggart, who had self-righteously condemned Bakker publicly, was discovered with a prostitute in Metairie, Louisiana.

"It's sad," lamented Billy. "The three men are so human."

Oral Roberts had overexpanded his university, and now

he was desperate beyond understanding by the public. Billy felt very sad about Oral's plight. But he had to call on his deepest reserve of Christian understanding to forgive the other two. All through his own ministry, First Corinthians 10 had reminded him that "God is faithful; he will not let you be tempted beyond what you can bear." But Billy was never foolish enough to push God. He knew he himself had to take precautions. He was never alone with another woman other than Ruth—ever.

All that misery was outdone by a great personal loss for Billy. Grady Wilson had been suffering from heart trouble for ten years. His activity had tailed off. But he still attended some of Billy's crusades. The Pillsbury Doughboy face couldn't be missed. Joy seemed to radiate away from it.

Grady cracked, "I'm ready to meet my Maker, but I ain't showing up ahead of time."

Yet everyone, including Grady, seemed to realize his stay in the hospital in fall 1987 was going to be his last. His unwavering cheery attitude proved to everyone how deep his faith was. At the funeral, Billy told what a great inspiration Grady's first sermon had been to him.

Billy always regretted how he overshadowed his cronies. He never felt more regret than at Grady's funeral. Grady had been a fine preacher. And he was the one who loosened up worriers like Lyndon Johnson and Richard Nixon with his barrage of humor. Besides Grady's contributions, his brother, T. W., was a wonderful organizer and expediter. Cliff Barrows was not only a song leader but a first-rate producer. It was Cliff who ramrodded the radio and television shows.

By 1988, evidence of illegal financial dealings by the

PTL Ministry was piling up. It was obvious that Bakker was going to be indicted. Equally as damaging to his image were revelations of his arrogance and love of power and money. Swaggart was caught a second time with a prostitute. He had tearfully appealed for forgiveness the first time on his own television show and managed to preserve his ministry. The second time was his undoing.

The press heaped scorn on televangelists. Even Billy's BGEA, which could not be considered an organization of televangelism at all, suffered. Billy's television specials were held four times a year, and he did not ask for money. He asked for hearts and souls. But many television news anchors tarred and feathered him with the others. As usual, Billy did not cry "foul." God would sort things out.

Beyond America, the world was changing. The Berlin Wall came down. Russian leader Gorbachev, lauding new policies of restructuring Russia called "perestroika" and openness called "glasnost," appeared to be sincere. And Billy achieved another goal: a crusade in Red China. He and Ruth, a "daughter of China," got a rousing welcome in the Great Hall of the People in Beijing. From there, Billy began a five-city crusade. He was cautious. As he had done previously in Communist countries, he emphasized that Christians were model citizens; that they should not be feared or persecuted. Second, he reassured Chinese Christians that they were part of a worldwide community of one billion Christians. Third, he pointed out that men must be at peace with God as well as the rest of mankind. Billy spent one hour with Premier Li Peng. On the way back to America, Billy was a guest of the Russian Orthodox Church in Moscow.

He still enjoyed influence with the White House. He attended state dinners, even the one for Gorbachev. He led prayers at both nominating conventions in the summer of 1988. George Bush, vice president under Reagan, was elected president. Billy was invited to give the prayer at his inaugural. In America, Billy continued citywide revivals, now cut back from eight-day to five-day crusades. And more and more, he became known internationally.

In 1989, he preached in Hungary again, this time in a stadium full of one hundred thousand nominal Communists. And his massive outreach called Mission World through satellite hookups was launched. From London, he spoke live to Britain, Ireland, and ten African countries. Delayed broadcasts were received by another twenty-three African countries. Detracting from Billy's efforts was the ongoing PTL scandal. Jimmy Bakker was sentenced to forty-five years in prison! In late 1990, Mission World eventually reached millions in Asia from Billy's live crusade in Hong Kong. Some were saying it reached one hundred million viewers. Billy was astonished by the magnitude of Mission World.

He told a reporter, "I feel like I'm ready to go to heaven. I never dreamed I would see a crusade like this." And he realized that he was echoing the Archbishop of Canterbury's words thirty-four years earlier. Where would it all stop?

America and Europe were preoccupied with the Middle East in 1990 and 1991. Armies of Iraq's maniacal dictator, Saddam Hussein, invaded Kuwait. It was a test of wills because Hussein clearly intended to invade Saudi Arabia next. That would have given the madman control of the majority of the world's production of oil. President Bush acted swiftly. He garnered the support of all the European allies and issued an ultimatum: Get out of Kuwait by January 15, 1991, or suffer the consequences. Hussein did not believe Bush.

The night of January 15, Billy and Ruth were at the White House. Bush, who was reluctant to speak openly about prayer because he wasn't sure how large a role religious beliefs should have in government, nevertheless always prayed for guidance. Billy helped him pray for peace. No sane person wanted a war.

Publicly Billy said, "Sometimes it is necessary to fight the bullies to protect the weak."

On January 16, a ferocious air attack on Iraq began and continued week after week. After Iraq had been numbed, Allied ground forces crushed the Iraqi armies in Kuwait. Even Russia had allied itself with the Western countries. The Gulf War seemed to be the forerunner of good news everywhere. Communism was unraveling all around the world at an astounding rate. The eastern European countries were ecstatic to shed Communism. Billy, criticized for being a dupe less than ten years earlier for saying spirituality and the spirit of freedom were alive and well in the Communist countries, was now seen as a visionary by the few who bothered to look back. The two Germanys reunited. And most shocking of all was the change in Russia. Communist Russia was dissolved by Gorbachev in 1991. Boris Yeltsin was the first president of the new "democratic" Russia.

At home, Billy followed up crusades of New Jersey and New York with a massive rally in Central Park. How could he ever top the Times Square rally of 1957? Yet, at the age of seventy-two, he did. The rally in New York's Central Park drew 250,000. His peaks seemed never to end. In November, he was in Buenos Aires preaching another chapter of Mission World, which relayed his sermons throughout Latin America.

In 1992, the organization Billy helped to found, the Evangelical Council for Financial Responsibility, or ECFR, showed how truly independent it was. It censured Franklin Graham for his activities with Samaritan's Purse and World Medical Mission, claiming he was overpaid, he used their aircraft for private use, and he pocketed large donations for himself. Billy and Ruth advised Franklin to withdraw his organizations from the ECFR, then reapply with his defense well documented. He did—with successful results.

At the end of March, for five days Billy penetrated the most recalcitrant Communist country in the world: North Korea. The leader was Kim Il Sung. As usual, Billy began by reassuring the leader that Christians were excellent citizens: sober, obedient, and industrious. He didn't have to point out that Christianity was thriving in South Korea, growing at a rate no one could have imagined just a decade earlier. Christianity was a force that had to be recognized in Asia.

Over the years, Billy had dealt with many illnesses: kidney stones, hernias, ulcers, tumors, polyps, hypertension, pneumonia, prostate trouble, and broken ribs. He didn't hide his complaints, either. With his usual frankness, he discussed them and didn't mind if his listener offered sympathy. He didn't get much from Ruth. She hid her illnesses like the great Livingstone of yesteryear and had scant sympathy for "hypochondriacs." But during the summer of 1992, even Ruth was stunned when Billy received the diagnosis of his latest affliction.

SEVENTEEN

Parkinson's Disease!" gasped Ruth.

Billy's symptoms of the progressive nervous disorder were tremors in his hands and fatigue. "God comes with greater power when we are weak," answered Billy to anyone who implied he should retire.

But he had to pause and reflect. His father, Frank, a non-smoking teetotaler who worked hard, lived to be seventy-four. Grandpa Crook Graham, a hardworking, heavy drinker, lived to be seventy. Grandpa Ben Coffey, more like Frank in his habits, lived to be seventy-three.

Billy was seventy-three. Even Ruth was impressed with the implications of the family tree. Billy decided he would slow down, just a bit. After all, he not only had nineteen grand-children, but he had five great-grandchildren.

He returned to Russia in October 1992. Finally, he could carry out a full-scale, citywide crusade. The eternal optimists of BGEA had reserved Moscow's indoor Olympic Stadium, which could hold 50,000. Turnouts averaged 45,000. The last night drew 50,000, with 20,000 standing outside. The number of inquirers was much higher than the usual 2 percent. It ran up to 25 percent. Cliff Barrows did not play the usual music; it only made the Russians flock to the altar dangerously fast.

"Please walk. Don't run," pleaded Billy. He had never seen such spiritual hunger. The Russians had been denied Christ for seventy-five years.

The overwhelming success of the Gulf War and the fall of Communism in Europe had a strange effect on the American people. They thought the world was no longer dangerous. It was high time to cut back defense and enjoy benefits at home. So who needed a president who was an expert on foreign affairs? Americans wanted someone sensitive to their own needs. In a shocking turnabout, they elected Bill Clinton, an obscure governor from Arkansas, who gained the nomination because the rest of the Democrats sat out the election, thinking Bush was unbeatable.

Billy's rapport with Clinton was strained. Clinton had snubbed an interview with *Christianity Today* before the election. After the election, the NRB, a group of evangelical broadcasters, invited Clinton to speak to their annual convention. Previous presidents had spoken to the group; Clinton did not even acknowledge the invitation. Instead, Clinton, who had campaigned as a "new" moderate Democrat, immediately pandered to liberal groups with lifestyles offensive to evangelicals. Nevertheless, Billy persisted in offering to help this new president, the most unreceptive since Truman.

In March 1993, Billy again preached over an extensive

satellite network, this time from Essen, Germany. The effort was now eight years old, and it was not just an attempt to reach millions upon millions of listeners. They had learned long ago that follow-up was critical. If counselors were not there to help inquirers, the effort was largely in vain. They now had to aim not so much at how many people they could reach but how many they could reach where counseling was at hand. The new direction called for a new name: Global Mission.

Billy thanked his key people. "How could we ever top this latest effort? Maybe that should be the last."

The mastermind of the satellite network, Bob Williams, muttered, "But we are just now learning to do it right."

Evangelizing continued by radio, television specials in prime time, satellite networking, magazines, movies, and citywide crusades like the one in Pittsburgh that summer. Billy had books generating royalties. And new evangelists were being trained all the time in America and abroad.

In 1994, Billy ventured into the Far East again. His four-day Tokyo crusade was the best ever in Japan for BGEA. He followed that success with ten days of preaching in Red China. Then he returned to North Korea. He delivered a message to Park Il Sung from President Clinton, who could make himself available when he needed a favor. This time Billy was allowed to preach in North Korea.

His citywide crusades in America were taking on a new flavor. He still preached as always but now supplemented the crusade with Youth Nights, characterized by Christian rock music. Notable was Franklin's entry in preaching at the citywide crusades. Billy knew that would cause speculation that

Franklin was about to take over the helm of BGEA. And someday Franklin would take over—but not yet. Besides, in his own mind, Billy felt BGEA could run itself. He had always delegated authority, and from top to bottom the organization was rife with competence.

"Look how Global Mission just gets bigger and bigger," said Billy. "I don't do anything."

In March 1995, Bob Williams implemented his latest version of Global Mission. It was colossal. From San Juan, Billy's three nights of sermons went to thirty satellites that sent them on to 185 countries. Only Red China did not participate. The telecasts were not intended to be live. Billy's thirty-minute sermons were translated into 116 languages and augmented by local gospel musicians and testimonials. Then tapes tailored to regional audiences were shown in three thousand sites with ten million seats! One million counselors were there waiting for the inquirers as they responded to the message of Christ. The effort did not end there. The tapes were to be shown to more and more sites in the months ahead.

The goal was to reach one billion people!

In June 1995, Billy collapsed at a luncheon in Toronto just before the five-day crusade was to begin. At seventy-six, he seemed constantly reminded now of his mortality. Billy's friends were falling one by one. Just the year before, he had spoken at Richard Nixon's funeral. Grady was gone. Cliff Barrows and Bev Shea had lost their wives. In Toronto, doctors discovered Billy was anemic due to a loss of blood. Cancer was ruled out. He recovered enough to preach at the fourth night of the crusade to a turnout of 73,500, the largest crowd ever at the Skydome.

In moments of exhaustion, Billy reflected on retiring. He felt fulfilled. Only God knew how many people he had preached to one way or another. The BGEA in Minneapolis was healthy. His school for evangelism at Wheaton was going strong. His center at Asheville was developing, even with the final resting place for Billy and Ruth already set aside. *Christianity Today* was a strong voice for evangelicals. His books numbered over a dozen with over ten million copies sold. More than any evangelist in history, he had fulfilled the "Great Commission" of Isaiah 49:6, expressed by Jesus Himself in Matthew 28:19: " 'Therefore go and make disciples of all nations, baptizing them in the name of the Father and of the Son and of the Holy Spirit.' "

And yet there were billions of souls out there to be saved. One of his fellow travelers he admired most also had reflected on retiring in tired and sickly moments: crusty old Dutch evangelist Corrie ten Boom. But she never did retire. She finally convinced herself God wanted her "to die in the harness." She continued preaching the gospel until her third stroke felled her. Even then, bedridden, she labored under the most frustrating disability to write devotionals. She died at ninety-one.

So, Billy, in failing health, would continue to evangelize. As he had said so many times, "I'll keep opening doors. God will sort it all out."

NOTES

CHAPTER 7

1. John Pollock, *Billy Graham: The Authorized Biography* (McGraw-Hill, 1966), 53.

CHAPTER 8

1. From *A Prophet with Honor* by William Martin. Copyright 1991 by William Martin. By permission of William Morrow & Co., Inc., 126.

CHAPTER 9

1. John Pollock, *Billy Graham: The Authorized Biography* (McGraw-Hill, 1966), 93.
2. Ibid., 99.

CHAPTER 10

1. John Pollock, *Billy Graham: The Authorized Biography* (McGraw-Hill, 1966), 122.
2. From *A Prophet with Honor* by William Martin. Copyright 1991 by William Martin. By permission of William Morrow & Co., Inc., 182.
3. Ibid., 182.
4. Charles T. Cook, *London Hears Billy Graham* (Marshall, Morgan and Scott, 1954), vii.
5. From *A Prophet with Honor* by William Martin. Copyright 1991 by William Martin. By permission of William Morrow & Co., Inc., 181.
6. Ibid., 223.

CHAPTER 11

1. From *A Prophet with Honor* by William Martin. Copyright 1991 by William Martin. By permission of William Morrow & Co., Inc., 190.
2. John Pollock, *Billy Graham: The Authorized Biography* (McGraw-Hill, 1966), 166.
3. From *A Prophet with Honor* by William Martin. Copyright 1991 by William Martin. By permission of William Morrow & Co., Inc., 216.

4. Ibid., 245.

5. Ibid., 246.

CHAPTER 12

1. Grady Wilson, *Count It All Joy* (Broadman Press, 1984), 296–297.

2. From *A Prophet with Honor* by William Martin. Copyright 1991 by William Martin. By permission of William Morrow & Co., Inc., 270.

3. John Pollock, *Billy Graham: The Authorized Biography* (McGraw-Hill, 1966), 216.

CHAPTER 13

1. John Pollock, *Billy Graham: The Authorized Biography* (McGraw-Hill, 1966), 234.

2. From *A Prophet with Honor* by William Martin. Copyright 1991 by William Martin. By permission of William Morrow & Co., Inc., 310.

CHAPTER 14

1. From *A Prophet with Honor* by William Martin. Copyright 1991 by William Martin. By permission of William Morrow & Co., Inc., 30.

2. Ibid., 351.

3. Ibid., 355.

4. Mary Bishop, *Billy Graham: The Man and the Ministry* (Grosset & Dunlap, 1978), 62.

CHAPTER 15

1. From *A Prophet with Honor* by William Martin. Copyright 1991 by William Martin. By permission of William Morrow & Co., 463.

CHAPTER 16

1. From *A Prophet with Honor* by William Martin. Copyright 1991 by William Martin. By permission of William Morrow & Co., 490.

HEROES OF THE FAITH

This exciting biographical series explores the lives of famous Christian men and women throughout the ages. These books will inspire and encourage you to follow the example of these "Heroes of the Faith" who made Christ the center of their existence.

208 pages / Only $1.99 each!

Amy Carmichael
Billy Graham
Corrie ten Boom
David Livingstone
Fanny Crosby
Florence Nightingale
Frederick Douglass
Free Indeed
Into All the World
Jim Elliot
Martin Luther
Well with My Soul

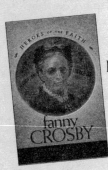

Available wherever books are sold.
Or order from:
Barbour Publishing, Inc.
P.O. Box 719
Uhrichsville, Ohio 44683
www.barbourbooks.com

If you order by mail, add $2.00 to your order for shipping.
Prices subject to change without notice.